THE CIVIL WAR IN SPAIN

3

THE
CIVIL
WAR
IN
SPAIN

by

Robert Goldston

LONDON : PHOENIX HOUSE

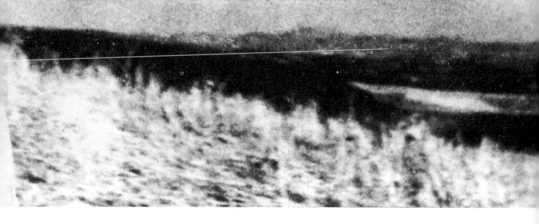

Illustrated with drawings by

Donald Carrick

Title-page photograph by Robert Capa—Magnum.
All other photographs supplied by United Press International.

ACKNOWLEDGMENTS

The author wishes to express his gratitude to Mr. W. H. Auden
and to Faber and Faber Ltd, for permission to quote from Mr.
Auden's poem 'Spain 1937', published by Faber and Faber Ltd,
in W. H. Auden's *Collected Poems 1930–1944*.

Copyright © 1966 by Robert Goldston
All rights reserved
Phototypeset by BAS Printers Ltd, Wallop, Hampshire
Made in Great Britain
by
Morrison & Gibb Ltd
London and Edinburgh
for
J. M. DENT & SONS LTD
Aldine House, Bedford Street, London, W.C.2.
A Phoenix House Publication
First published in Great Britain 1967.

Al Pueblo de
Santa Eulalia del Río

CONTENTS

Spain, July, 1936

Prologue

FIRST of all, there is the land itself—a land of great contrasts. In most places the soil is hard, unyielding; some have called it cruel. In the north are arid, stony hills; in the center, high, windy plateaus; in the south, large desert regions. Throughout most of the Iberian Peninsula the land wages endless war against all who try to wrest a living from it. Water is very scarce, and against most horizons the land erupts into huge mountain ranges. The hills are dotted by tiny stone villages, each clustered tenaciously around its crumbling church, where life is lived at the same pace and with almost the same harshness as it was lived centuries ago. Water is still drawn from the village well, light is still supplied by candles, stoves are still fired by wood, and time is measured by the slow cycle of Saints' Days on the church calendar.

But certain river valleys of the south and the Mediterranean Coast are subtropical gardens. There the land is rich and water abundant. It is there, in Andalusia, that Spain's great export crops are raised: olives, figs, oranges, and almonds. The land is divided into great, almost feudal estates. There are huge cattle ranches and vast vineyards—and sparkling white adobe-walled villages where the backbreaking toil of the day explodes into the fierce gaiety of *flamenco* rhythms at night.

There are coal and iron in the north, as well as some lead, zinc, and silver, but barely enough to support Spain's light industry. Most heavy industrial goods are imported. Electricity is drawn from the great rivers—the Ebro, the Guadalquivir, and the Tagus. But there are still lightless hours during the summer droughts in Madrid and Barcelona.

Spain is almost completely surrounded by the sea, and its fishing industry is a large one. From the great port cities of Bilbao, Barcelona, Valencia, Vigo, and Cadiz a modest international trade is carried on. But apart from the Basques, the Galicians, and the Catalans in the north, the Spaniard is not a seafaring man. Since the time of the Invincible Armada, Spain has not been pre-eminent upon the seas.

A hard land, a poor country—but a nation rich in human resources, rich in spirit. The Spanish temper has been forged on a hard anvil and is as extreme as the geography that has shaped it. And although it is never wise to generalize about a people (especially a nation of thirty million individualists), the Spaniard has revealed several qualities of spirit so persistently that they might almost be called national characteristics.

First of all, there is courage—the courage of the small band of Christian knights who would not bow before the power of Islam and eventually defeated it in a war that lasted over seven hundred years; the courage of the handful of conquistadors who discovered, explored, and conquered a new world from the mighty Indian empires of Central and South America; the courage of the officers and men who took their under-equipped, outclassed, and outnumbered ships into action against powerful American squadrons in 1898. This courage, shown equally on both sides of the Spanish Civil War battle lines, was to catch and hold the admiration of the world in our own times.

Secondly, there is a fierce spirit of independence in the Spaniard. He is the straight-backed old *hidalgo* who would sooner starve than accept alms; the crusading knight who prefers death to defeat; and the temperamental statesman too proud to compromise, even though his country faces ruin. This deep-rooted individualism has made many Spaniards great (one thinks of El Cid, Cortés, Pizarro, Balboa, Cervantes, Velásquez, Picasso), but it has time and again brought ruin to the nation and kept the country a battlefield for centuries.

Thirdly, the Spaniard is an idealist of the most extreme variety; he has as much contempt for half-hearted emotions as for lightly held convictions. He may be the most religious of Catholics or the most revolutionary of anarchists. He is the world's most pious saint and the world's most ferocious fighter. He is Father Junípero Serra working himself to death to help the Indian tribes of California, and he is also Philip the Second, launching armies and fleets to enslave Protestant Europe. Sometimes he is both, as was Saint Ignatius Loyola who founded the militant Society of Jesus. During the Civil War the Spaniard was the priest who suffered death rather than give up his religion, and he was also the unarmed peasant who threw himself against machine guns for revolutionary ideals.

Gaiety and humor are part of the Spanish character, too. It is said that there are more *fiestas* on the Spanish calendar than days in the year. And the Spaniard can laugh at himself, at his fiery temperament—it was Miguel de Cervantes, after all, who poked most fun at that temperament in *Don Quixote de la Mancha.*

What has been the history of this formidable people? Briefly, it has been one of conquest and war. First came the Phoenicians, carrying the trade of ancient Egypt and the Middle East to the wild Iberian tribes of the peninsula, and establishing ports at places such as Alicante and Valencia. Then came the Carthaginians from North Africa, who conquered much of Spain and used it as a base in their wars against Rome. When Hannibal led his elephants over the Alps to march on Rome he had regiments of Iberian infantry and Balearic stone slingers in his army; in fact, Hannibal was born in Spain, and his father, Hamilcar Barca, founded the great city of Barcelona. But when Carthage lost her struggle against Rome she lost her Spanish colony as well.

The Romans came, bringing roads, laws, aqueducts, and arenas in the wake of Cato's legions and imposing their own Latin language, which has developed into modern Spanish. The Roman rule was long. Beneath the imperial banners the Iberian tribes were civilized so successfully that they eventually supplied emperors to Rome itself. And while Saint Peter was being crucified on Vatican Hill, Saint James (in Spanish "Santiago") was, according to Spanish legend, bringing Christianity to Spain.

The fall of Rome brought Visigoth barbarians to the Iberian Peninsula. But these fierce tribes, like conquerors before and since, were soon civilized by the conquered and converted to Christianity. They set up many petty independent kingdoms throughout the land as the Dark Ages settled over Europe. But they were not to enjoy their dominion long—for far to the east Mohammed had raised the banner of holy war against Christendom.

Once again a great invading army descended on Spain from Africa. This time it was composed of Moors, a mighty tribe of Moslem warriors who soon conquered most of the land for Islam. Riding swift white Arabian chargers, wielding flashing scimitars, and employing cavalry tactics unknown to Europe, this race of fanatic fighters easily destroyed the Visigoth kingdom and drove Christianity back to the foothills of the Pyrenees.

But once in control, the Moors proceeded to build in Spain the greatest civilization of Medieval Europe. They irrigated the land and converted deserts into gardens. They built beautiful palaces and cities such as Granada, Seville, and Cordova. They founded universities where such subjects as algebra, astronomy, medicine, and philosophy were studied while the rest of the Western world remained largely illiterate. It seemed indeed as if the Moors had come to stay.

Yet in the far north, among the arid hills, the shattered Christians refused to surrender. Divided by the jealousies of petty kings, abandoned by the rest of Catholic Europe, controlling only a small area of their former homeland, these rough knights and peasants kindled the flame of a crusade to reconquer their country. The struggle was long, complicated, and seemingly hopeless. The story of their greatest champion, El Cid, was one of defeat as well as victory and of betrayal by his own king. But in the face of all obstacles and at the expense of generations of lives, after a series of wars which continued for more than seven centuries, Christian Spain triumphed. In 1492 Queen Isabella and King Ferdinand conquered the last Moorish stronghold and united their country beneath the banners of Castile and Aragon. It was, in fact, upon this very field of victory, encamped beneath the walls of fallen Granada, that Columbus finally received his commission to sail on a voyage of discovery across the western seas.

And now began the age of Spanish greatness. Her explorers opened up a vast new empire in the Americas while her armies swept all before them in Europe's complicated wars. The great Aztec Empire of Mexico fell to Cortés and a few followers; in Peru, the Incas surrendered to Pizarro and a handful of adventurers. Spanish fleets ruled the oceans, bringing to the homeland gold and silver from the New World, conquering the remote Philippine Islands, and making the Mediterranean Sea into a Spanish lake. And if this was an age of conquest, it was also an age of faith. The Spanish saw their wars both overseas and in Europe as a continuation of their holy crusade against the Moors. Wherever they went, from the steaming jungles of South America to the rich cities of Holland, they fought to implant and enforce the Catholic faith.

But conquest often carries the seeds of its own destruction. As the wealth of the world flowed into Spanish vaults, her people lost their taste for work. Why should the peasant toil to scratch a living from the soil when the plunder of rich cities could be won with a sword? Why should the *hidalgo* tend his estates when he could carve himself out a princely realm in distant lands? Why should the government worry about home industries when the mines of Mexico poured forth their endless treasures? A country exhausted by hundreds of years of war found itself committed not only to the conquest of distant continents but also to wage war against all of Protestant Europe to defend Catholicism against the Reformation. Inevitably, disaster came.

At home, the worn-out land could no longer support huge armies or great fleets. Philip the Second, greatest of all Spanish monarchs, lived to see his armies defeated in Holland and his Invincible Armada scattered by the English in the Channel. The defense of the overseas colonies grew increasingly difficult. There were constant Indian rebellions, and Spanish colonists paid little heed to orders from Madrid. The manhood and treasure of Spain were drained away by imperial ambition and religious fervor. During the two centuries following the Armada, Spain's international position, reflecting her internal weakness, declined until she found herself a mere pawn in the brutal game of European power politics.

Spain's international prestige reached perhaps its lowest ebb during the reign of Charles IV (1788–1808), a dull, amiable, and indifferent monarch wholly ruled by his ambitious wife, Maria Luisa of Parma, and her lover Manuel de Godoy, an officer she raised to Prime Minister at the age of twenty-five. Clumsily attempting to steer a safe course through the storm of the French Revolution and the Napoleonic conquest of Europe, Godoy and the monarchy succeeded only in losing to France the vast Louisiana Territory (which Napoleon proceeded to sell to the United States in defiance of treaty obligations to Spain), and involving Spain in Napoleon's wars against England. Thus, a Spanish fleet shared the French disaster at Trafalgar, and Spain was reduced to accepting the passage of French armies through her territory on their way to the conquest of Portugal. Godoy, who enthusiastically supported Napoleon's attack on Portugal in hopes of carving himself a principality from that kingdom, soon found that French forces "passing through" Spain were in fact occupying the country. When Godoy protested to Napoleon, the French Emperor merely replied, "Is the King of Spain tired of reigning?" But he later withdrew the troops.

The respite was only temporary, however. For in November of 1807, French Army corps crossed the Pyrenees for still another attack on Portugal, and in the following year additional forces were sent that occupied all of northern Spain. Napoleon's Army in Spain had now swelled to 100,000 men, and his intentions could no longer be doubted. Meeting no opposition, the French seized Madrid. From the weak Charles IV (who, with his wife Maria Luisa, his son Ferdinand, and the conniving Godoy, found himself a prisoner in France), Napoleon wrung an act of abdication. The Emperor promptly named his own brother Joseph King of Spain.

But if he held the Spanish monarchy in contempt, Napoleon had not reckoned with the Spanish people. In spite of their disgust with Charles IV, the people of Spain could not support this insult to national pride. On the second of May, 1808, the populace of

Madrid rose in bloody rebellion against French occupying forces. Although the uprising was quickly and savagely suppressed in the capital, it ignited a spark that soon engulfed all of Spain in the fire of revolution against the detested French.

The *Dos de Mayo* (May 2) has been held ever since as Spain's proudest hour. Although he might be fighting for the wrong ends in some respects, and on behalf of a monarchy he himself detested, nevertheless the Spaniard was to find himself in the fires of war once again, to prove that even at this lowest point of his nation's fortunes he remained a man and not a chattel. His formidable will was soon demonstrated by Spanish victories at Bailén and Saragossa during the summer of 1808. Joseph "the Intruder" had to flee from Madrid after a reign of ten days in July of 1808, and Napoleon himself, with an army numbering 300,000 men, was forced to come to Spain to restore Joseph to the throne.

Against this overwhelming force, the Spaniards appealed for help to England, the old enemy. English troops under Sir Arthur Wellesley (later Duke of Wellington) were dispatched to the Iberian Peninsula and, in conjunction with the Spaniards, waged a seesaw series of campaigns against the French, mightily aided by the nationwide *guerrilla* (little war) carried on by the Spanish masses against their oppressors. For six years the struggle was unremitting—but it was crowned with triumph when, in 1813, Joseph fled across the Pyrenees. In the following year the last pockets of French resistance were wiped out, and Wellington marched north into France. Within fifteen days after the last French surrender in Spain, Napoleon found his empire reduced to the island of Elba—and the constant drain of the Spanish campaigns had contributed to that end as much as his disastrous invasion of Russia.

But meanwhile, with their king a prisoner in France, the Spanish people had ruled themselves through local *juntas* (councils) and become aware that they held their destiny in their own hands.

Thus, in 1810, the *juntas* of Andalusia had summoned a national *Cortes* (parliament) to meet at Cadiz. There, after much debate, a regency was declared for the absent king. In 1812, a national constitution was proclaimed that gave the *Cortes* legislative powers and limited the authority of the monarchy. Thus, while the French were being defeated in the field, French ideas of popular sovereignty won a lasting foothold in the Spanish mind.

When Ferdinand (Charles IV's son) returned in triumph to Spain in 1814 as Ferdinand VII, he soon made it apparent that he had no intention of honoring the constitution established during his absence. Consequently, liberal elements of the Army revolted in 1820 in an attempt to force a liberal regime on the king. But Ferdinand, appealing to the re-established Bourbon monarchy in France, was able to summon help. One hundred thousand French troops—styling themselves "the hundred thousand sons of Saint Louis"—restored Ferdinand's power and crushed the rebellion.

And while Ferdinand's reactionary policies kept Spain in turmoil at home, his provocative colonial policy was rewarded by a wave of revolution among the Spanish overseas colonies. By 1825 the last Spanish colony in continental South and Central America had won its independence.

The tyranny of Ferdinand VII was made only barely tolerable to the Spanish people, especially the Basques and Catalans in the north, by the prospect that upon his death, his brother Don Carlos, who promised local home rule to Catalonia and the Basque provinces, would succeed to the throne. But, in 1830, Ferdinand's third wife, Maria Cristina of Naples, bore him a daughter. Disregarding the old Spanish law that held that a woman could not succeed to the Spanish throne, Ferdinand, at the instigation of his ambitious wife, announced that his daughter Isabella would succeed him. Thus, when Ferdinand died in 1833, the infant Isabella II was proclaimed Queen under the regency of her mother, Maria Cristina. This was too much for Don Carlos and his followers, and in 1834 they rose in the first of the civil wars known as the Carlist Wars, which were to rend the fabric of Spanish life for much of the nineteenth century.

To add to the confusion, it turned out that Maria Cristina, as Regent for Isabella II, was, in spite of a personal life steeped in scandal, of liberal leanings. Her rule was constitutional and in some respects even anticlerical (the property of most religious orders in Spain was seized by her government in 1836, for example). Thus, the supporters of Don Carlos soon came to include the more reactionary and absolutist elements of Spanish life, while the forces fighting for the queen could be seen as the liberals.

By 1839, under the leadership of General Baldomero Espartero, the Carlists had been defeated throughout Spain. In 1841, with the Queen Mother Maria Cristina sent into exile, General Espartero proclaimed himself Regent. But amid the kaleidoscope of intrigues and plots surrounding the throne, Espartero found himself forced from power in 1843 when Isabella II was proclaimed of age to rule. Her reign, which was to last until 1868, was marked by incessant local uprisings, insubordination on the part of various generals, unnecessary and unprofitable wars with Peru and Chile, and finally, nationwide revolution in 1868.

In that year, led by General Juan Prim (who had won glory by defeating the Riff tribesmen of Morocco in 1860), the Army, with widespread popular support, forced Isabella II into exile and proclaimed yet another regency. Amadeus, Duke of Aosta, was invited to accept the Spanish crown in 1871, but so uneasily did it sit on his head that after two years he abdicated to follow his predecessors into exile.

With the throne vacant and years of disorder behind them, the Spanish people turned at last to the experiment of a republic. In 1873, a republic was proclaimed, and under the leadership of such men as Estanislao Figueras, Francisco Pí y Margall, and

Emilio Castelar y Ripoll, the *Cortes* attempted to rule the country directly along constitutional lines.

But in that same year of 1873, exasperated by the continuing fluctuations of government, the Carlists once again rose to plunge the nation into a second Carlist War. The disorders and anarchy were so widespread that the Army abolished the Republican government and, in an attempted compromise, restored Isabella II's son Alfonso XII to the Spanish throne in 1874. With the Carlists once again defeated by 1876, Alfonso's reign proceeded along constitutional lines. Under the guidance of Prime Minister Antonio Canovas del Castillo, his government strove for peace and, above all, order.

Upon Alfonso XII's death in 1885, his wife Maria Cristina of Hapsburg-Lorraine was declared Regent for the infant Alfonso XIII. It was during her rule, in 1898, that Spain's last important overseas colonies, Cuba, Puerto Rico, and the Philippines, fell prey to an expansionist United States.

Thus, at the dawn of a new century and a new reign (Alfonso XIII was declared of age and proclaimed King in 1902) Spain found herself, after a century of incessant disorder, bloodshed, and civil war, reduced to a third-rate power internationally and suffering from unhealed wounds internally. Spanish intellectuals of the rising generation known as the Generation of '98 realized that their country desperately needed peace abroad, industrialization at home, and a stable, liberal, and progressive government. But how to achieve these things? Many solutions were offered, and it was the failure of each and all of them that was to lead to the most terrible of all of Spain's civil wars.

I

How War Came

THE shifting vagaries of politics in Spain—the game of exiling kings, of seizures of power by generals and admirals, of "fixing" elections to the moribund *Cortes*—and, in fact, the entire spectrum of Spanish political activity during the nineteenth and part of the twentieth centuries were only the reflection of a desperate attempt by a small handful of Spaniards to stop the clock of progress, to preserve a society in which their privileges and great wealth would remain inviolate at whatever cost to the great mass of the people. To the landowners and aristocrats who could buy and sell elections and who ran their estates as if they were feudal domains of the fifteenth century, to the bishops and higher officials of the Catholic Church who enjoyed a control over Spanish life in all its phases such as had been seen in no other nation since the Reformation, to the generals and admirals who had come to regard themselves as an indispensable power within the state and whose activities were much more political than military, the sometimes constitutional, often corrupt, and always inefficient monarchy provided an admirable screen behind which to exploit the Spanish people. And since they controlled the wealth and the fighting forces of the nation, their influence was great, their power apparently unassailable.

Yet behind this facade of power, the same ideas that stirred men everywhere were gaining ground—feeding on the very oppression that was designed to suppress them. First and historically foremost among these was the idea of a republic. In spite of the betrayal and suppression of the Constitution of 1812, in spite of the chaos that had engulfed the short-lived Republic of 1873, the idea of a republic still burned brightly among certain classes. To the intellectuals of the universities, the small landowners, some junior officers in both the Army and the Navy, the lower middle classes generally, the republican solution seemed to promise a rational way out of the reactionary corruption that frustrated all their hopes. After overthrowing the monarchy and proclaiming Spain a republic they proposed to legislate their country into the twentieth century. They would give the vote to everyone and make certain the vote was meaningful by strict control over elections; separate the Church and state, removing education from Church control, confiscating some of the vast holdings of convents and monasteries, and proclaiming religious liberty throughout the land; redistribute the land to raise up a class of small, independent farmers in place of the enslaved peasants who toiled on the great estates; reduce the Army to proper proportion in national life; and, in general, establish the kind of political and economic system familiar in the United States.

But the history of Spain had not been the history of the United States. In place of a rich continent to exploit, here was an exhausted country. In place of an ancient code of common law to protect personal liberty, Spain had a tradition of rule by the strongest and law made at the whim of the powerful. Could Spain afford a republic at this late date? Could her semi-literate masses be educated to rule themselves? Could her proud temperament lend itself to the arts of compromise and persuasion in place of fanatical fervor? Many middle-class Spaniards believed it possible. But as their numbers were few, their strength was based primarily upon the power of their ideas—and these ideas were contested from below as well as from above.

Throughout the centuries one fact of Spanish life had never changed. This was the terrible fact of grinding poverty for the great mass of Spanish workers and peasants. At the beginning of the twentieth century, the peasants still labored under feudal conditions on huge estates, the owners of which were usually to be found enjoying the comforts of Madrid, London, or Paris. The Spanish *grandee* did not consider himself responsible for either the productivity of his land or the welfare of the workers on it. So long as it maintained him in idleness and luxury he cared nothing for the fortunes of his estate. The attitude of the Spanish aristocracy towards the masses from whom they drew their wealth was similar to that of the French aristocracy on the eve of the French Revolution—and the consequences were as drastic.

The condition of the workers in the cities was only slightly better than that of the peasants. Where the peasant was almost always completely illiterate, the factory worker could often read and write; where the peasant earned perhaps sixpence a day, the factory worker might earn as much as one and threepence. But, of course, prices were higher in the cities. The industrial slums that grew on the outskirts of Bilbao, Barcelona, and Madrid were as horrible as any the Western world had to show.

It was no wonder, then, that the workers and peasants of Spain (and they were the overwhelming majority) sought more radical solutions to social problems than the middle classes. Two great movements developed at the turn of the century—anarchism among the peasants and socialism among the workers. Both of these movements were part of world-wide attempts to solve some of the problems arising from the Industrial Revolution.

Anarchism appealed to the peasants because of its easily understood aims. To the Anarchists, all government (since it was based on the idea of authority and force) was morally wrong. It should be swept away—by revolution if necessary. In place of government, the Anarchists would organize very small self-governing bodies such as factory councils and village committees. These small units in turn would make whatever agreements were necessary between them to further the general welfare. There would be no police, no army to enforce their decisions; everything would be voluntary and cooperative. But in Spain anarchism developed into something more extreme, more religiously fanatic, than anywhere else in the world. Anarchist organizers would arrive at some small Andalusian village, organize schools for the peasants, preach their doctrines, and then go on to organize crusades against alcoholic drink, meat-eating, smoking, and faithlessness to wives. In many places they even taught the evil effects of coffee and tea drinking! But the Anarchists' extremism took more violent forms also. As the movement grew into millions it found itself the object of ruthless attacks by the frightened Army and police. The Anarchists' response was twofold. In the cities they developed the strike as a political weapon. A call from Anarchist leaders would bring every single worker in an entire city out on strike. Besides that, they organized a very large force of terrorists. These men (there were about fifty thousand of them) would shoot down their enemies, blow up factories and trains, lead peasants in burning landlords' houses, and commit any violent action that would either terrify their enemies or attract attention to their program. In keeping with Anarchist ideals, the Spanish Anarchist movement was only loosely organized—but it had by far the largest following in Spain.

The Socialists, who traced their origins to the teachings of Karl Marx, were very much opposed to Anarchist ideas. Socialists believed that the means of production—the factories, farms, mines, mills, and shipyards—should be owned and operated by the people who worked in them. The government, too, should be run entirely by workers for the benefit of workers. This would, of course, mean that the middle class, the aristocracy, the monarchy, and the Church would have to be dispossessed. Many Spanish Socialists thought they could accomplish this through reforms and constitutional means. They put their faith in educating the people to what they believed were their true interests, striking for better wages and conditions, electing representatives to the *Cortes* who would vote for their program. But there were some among the Spanish Socialists who did not believe that the great landowners, the factory operators, the Church, and the monarchy could be eliminated by such peaceful means. These dissenting Socialists predicted and worked for a revolution—although they were against the Anarchists' terrorist tactics.

The success of the Russian Revolution was later to lead to the formation of an even more extreme leftist organization—the Spanish Communist Party—which found itself more and more under the control of Russia and remained for many years small and insignificant. Later, following the ideological wars of the parent party in Russia, the Spanish Communist Party split into two parts —with the Trotskyists (who believed in world-wide and permanent revolution as opposed to national revolution) setting up a splinter party of their own. The Trotskyist branch of the Communist movement in Spain was to develop a large following— especially in Barcelona.

The two major parties of the left—the Socialists and the Anarchists—thus disagreed violently about how the nation should be organized, but they agreed on several important matters. They both felt, for instance, that capitalism had no future in Spain. They saw no benefit in the people exchanging an aristocratic set of masters for a middle-class set of masters. And they were both anticlerical—that is to say, they were both against the organization of the Catholic Church in Spain, though they may not have been antireligious. And this was a vitally important question to the people of Spain.

There had never been a Reformation in Spain. The Catholic Church had remained, since the days of the Moors, the single most powerful, the most united, and the richest institution in the entire country. Over the years the workers and peasants began to feel that the Church always supported the wealthy and neglected the poor. It was true that the Church supported the monarchy, the landlords, and the Army, but very many of the parish priests and some of the bishops championed the poor. Still, the high officials —the cardinals and archbishops—were very reactionary. They looked upon all efforts at reform, no matter where they arose, as work of the Devil. When the Pope advised them to liberalize, they paid little heed; they considered themselves more Catholic than the Pope.

The great majority of Spanish peasants and workers remained deeply religious even though they grew anticlerical. They were not against the teachings of the Church so much as they were against many of its officers. In true Spanish fashion, they hated hypocrisy. For example, if a parish priest wore his best clothes to the funeral of a rich man but dressed shabbily for the funeral of a poor man, that priest risked death and the burning of his church—not for being a priest, but for not living up to the teachings of Christ.

Another political concept that had long been powerful in certain sections of Spain was separatism. To the industrialized people of Catalonia and the Basque provinces, it seemed very evident that they would do far better to manage their own affairs than to continue to submit to the central authority of Madrid—no matter what form that authority took, whether monarchy, republic, or dictatorship. In many respects their interests were opposed to those of the agricultural south, and commercially as well as intellectually they felt stronger ties with France and western Europe than with Castile and Andalusia. They continued to agitate for autonomy within the Spanish state—some for complete independence. Basque hopes for autonomy, it will be remembered, had been an important factor in the bitter Carlist Wars of the nineteenth century. No reorganization of Spanish life could fail to come to terms with separatist sentiment.

/ Such were the divisions among the Spanish people as they entered the twentieth century. On the right were the Army, Church, monarchy, aristocracy, and landlords—all supporting the old order and resisting change. On the left were the great masses of peasants and workers who demanded change and expected that a violent revolution would be necessary to achieve it. And caught in the middle were the Republicans and Liberals, a minority placing their faith in reason and persuasion.

By 1921 the quarrels among the Spanish political parties, with general strikes, assassinations, riots, and disorders on the left, and lockouts, police brutality, corruption, and Army massacres of peasants and workers on the right, had brought the government of Alfonso XIII to the brink of disaster. What finally pushed it over that brink was the terrible defeat suffered by the Spanish Army in Morocco that year. Caught by the Riff tribesmen led by Abd-el-Krim at Anual in Morocco, the entire Spanish Moroccan Army of twenty thousand men was almost annihilated. Army corruption and inefficiency were clearly to blame. Government attempts to cover up the truth regarding this disaster only enraged the Spanish people more. An investigation was forced upon the unwilling Alfonso XIII. In spite of delays that lasted almost two years and endless attempts to suppress evidence, it soon became apparent that the government of Alfonso XIII would not be able to protect the Army, corrupt government ministers, and the king himself from the nation's wrath once the Anual report was made public. The Army decided to act.

Sure of the support of his brother officers, General Miguel Primo de Rivera, Captain-General of Catalonia, early in 1923 sent a telegram to Alfonso XIII demanding that he be made dictator. Primo de Rivera warned the king that the Army was behind him and threatened civil war if Alfonso refused. "Today we are resolved on moderation," the telegram stated, "but on the other hand we shall not shrink from bloodshed."

Primo de Rivera's threats were not really necessary. Alfonso XIII was only too happy to suspend the constitution and rule through this strong general. Seven very strange years followed. Once, on a state visit to Rome, Alfonso XIII introduced Primo de Rivera to King Victor Emmanuel of Italy as "my Mussolini." But Primo de Rivera was very far from being a Mussolini. He was not even a Fascist. True, he acted as a dictator. Political opponents were imprisoned, and he relied upon armed might to support himself. But he did not enjoy or manipulate a large mass following such as brought Mussolini, and later Hitler, to power. He had no theories about race, made no mystique out of war or force, waged no battle against intellect or religion, and had no ambitions for foreign conquest. In fact, he brought the colonial wars in Morocco to an end with final victory over Abd-el-Krim in 1925. He did suppress strikes, start a huge road-building program, and abolish the *Cortes*. He was a "strong man" in the old tradition of Spanish generals. Of course, his task was made easier by the fact that during the 1920's Spain, like all the rest of Europe, was enjoying prosperity.

Primo de Rivera's government was so personal it reflected almost exactly the character of the man himself. He was brave, patriotic, and very given to dramatic gestures. It is said that he once went to a theater in Madrid and started smoking, although smoking was forbidden. When one of his aides mentioned this to him, Primo de Rivera arose, flourished his cigar, and proclaimed to the audience, "Tonight, everybody may smoke!" He was a hard worker but also a hard drinker. He would disappear from Madrid for days at a time only to be found enjoying himself among the gypsies.

Primo's downfall in Spain was caused by the world-wide financial Depression of the thirties. In 1930 the dictator's corrupt financial structure collapsed and his government deserted him. He sent a telegram to Army garrisons all over Spain asking if they would continue to support him. When he learned they would not, Primo de Rivera fled to Paris where he died soon afterwards.

Now King Alfonso XIII tried to return to constitutional rule. But there were few people left in Spain who supported him. The Church had no confidence that he would protect it from the Anarchists, the Army considered him personally dishonorable, the Socialists and Liberals hated him in any case. In the autumn of 1930 the Republicans and Socialists finally signed an agreement to work together to abolish the monarchy. Deserted by everyone, Alfonso was forced to call for municipal elections. When the results of these elections became known on April 12, 1931, it was evident he could not remain upon the throne. "Sunday's elections," he announced, "have shown me that I no longer enjoy the love of my people [this was one of the great understatements of history]. . . . Until the nation speaks, I shall deliberately suspend the use of my royal prerogatives," he concluded, thereby not *quite* abdicating. But the result was the same. For with these weak words the last of Spain's kings fled Madrid for exile in Rome, where he was to die ten years later.

The liberal Republicans were in raptures. The monarchy had been overthrown without bloodshed. On April 14, 1931, a republic was declared. A provisional government with Niceto Alcalá Zamora as President and Prime Minister took over the government ministries in Madrid that same day to the cheers of thousands. Now the Republicans would proceed to create a democracy in Spain. But their optimism was, to say the least, premature.

First of all, there remained the great mass of peasants—overwhelmingly Anarchist. Although pleased to see the king flee, the Anarchists wanted no government at all. They would continue to carry out their program of strikes, political assassinations, and terrorism against the Republican government as they had against the monarchy.

Secondly, there was the Catholic Church to consider. The powerful bishops who drew strength not only from entrenched position but also from the sway they exercised over the minds of millions of Spaniards (especially the women of Spain) were willing to tolerate the Republic if they had to, but only if it did not interfere with their ancient rights and privileges.

Thirdly, there was the Army—also reluctantly prepared to give the Republic a chance to prove itself, but with a century-old tradition of interfering in political affairs and a naturally conservative outlook.

Finally, there were the separatists of Catalonia and the Basque provinces to consider. With the establishment of the Republic, Catalans and Basques took for granted the establishment of autonomous home rule in their regions. But any government in Madrid that allowed too much autonomy to these sections ran a serious risk of provoking the Army to action.

Still, the Republic might have survived all this had conditions in Spain given it time. Here were a group of idealists—men who had been university professors, lawyers, poets, writers—with very little political experience, trying to erect in Spain something similar to an American or English democracy. But in Spain there was no tradition of democratic rule, no educated mass of people to make wise elective choices, and, above all, no middle class worthy of the name on which to base large political parties. In Spain there were only the very rich and the very poor—and neither had any confidence in the government.

A series of bloody incidents illustrated this even before the new constitution had been worked out.

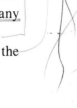

On May 10, 1931 (less than a month after the proclamation of the Republic), a group of Army officers met in a house on Calle Alcalá, one of Madrid's main streets. Faced with the reality of a Republican government, they were prepared to plot its overthrow and to restore Alfonso XIII to the throne. They made no secret of their meeting, and a large crowd gathered on the street outside. A group of officers arriving late by taxi mistook the crowd for supporters and shouted, "Viva la Monarquía!" The taxi driver immediately shouted back, "Viva la República!" One of the officers struck him, and the crowd assumed that he had been killed. The mob set fire to the house in which the Monarchist officers were gathered and then stormed through Madrid, setting fire to a Monarchist newspaper office and wrecking churches. "The justice of the people on thieves!" was a slogan chalked on the ruins of one of Madrid's central churches. Within a few days antimonarchist and antichurch rioting spread throughout Spain. Churches were burned in Andalusia and Catalonia. While the officers' plot evaporated, the Republican government seemed unable or unwilling to control these mobs. The new Minister of War, Manuel Azaña, said he would prefer to see buildings destroyed rather than Republicans harmed.

It was in this atmosphere that the provisional government of Alcalá Zamora called for nationwide elections to a national *Cortes*. These elections, conducted fairly and without violence, returned 114 Socialists, 145 Republicans, 56 Radical Socialists, 28 Rightist Republicans, 19 Conservatives, and 1 Monarchist to the *Cortes*. This was obviously an overwhelming Socialist-Republican victory, and, confident of the support of the people, the new *Cortes* proceeded to frame a constitution for the Spanish Republic.

The new constitution provided for equality before the law; renunciation of war as an instrument of national policy; universal suffrage for men and women above the age of twenty-three; abolition of all titles of nobility; the disestablishment of Catholicism

Manuel Azaña

as the official religion and the withdrawal of all government support for the Church as well as the ending of Church authority over education; the establishment of free and compulsory primary education; and, finally, the right for any region of Spain to apply to the *Cortes* for a statute of autonomy, although no completely autonomous regions were to be permitted.

In many respects this constitution was very similar to the Constitution of 1812. But in its present context it had serious drawbacks. First and foremost was its granting of the vote to women. It was notorious in Spain that the overwhelming majority of Spanish women would probably vote as their priests dictated. Then the disestablishment of the Catholic Church, while long overdue, was something that could not be effected simply by a stroke of the pen, while the withdrawal of government support could only serve to enrage the hierarchy. The abolition of Church-controlled education was a serious matter in a country where such education was the only type available for the great majority of the people. The renunciation of war as a national policy, while not in itself objectionable to an army well aware of its inability to wage a foreign war, nevertheless provoked the generals and admirals by its clear intimation of the downgrading of Army and Navy influence and prestige in the new state. The ambiguous solution to the separatist claims left the question of autonomy unsolved.

The new constitution was, nonetheless, approved by the *Cortes* on December 9, 1931, and the following day Alcalá Zamora was chosen President with Manuel Azaña as his Prime Minister.

The career of the first Republican government was, from the outset, a stormy one. The removal of Church influence and local government in Spanish life proved easier to decree than to carry out. No new answers were found to the continuance of Anarchist strikes in the cities; and protracted delay over the question of land reform cost the government important popular support among the peasants. A statute of autonomy was passed in the *Cortes* for Catalonia, but it was far weaker than the Catalans had hoped for, and their disillusionment went deep. A corresponding statute for the Basques, although submitted in 1932, was delayed for years— until after the Civil War had disrupted the fabric of the nation.

The impatience with which the Spanish peasantry viewed the endless delays of the new government in making immediate and apparent changes in their daily lives was brutally illustrated by a terrible incident that took place on December 31, 1931.

In the remote, wild hills of Estremadura, in a tiny village called Castilblanco, the Anarchists decided to hold a meeting. The government in Madrid refused them permission. The Anarchists went ahead anyhow. The local garrison of the *Guardia Civil* proceeded then, on instructions from Madrid, to break up the meeting.

The *Guardia Civil,* half police, half national guardsmen, were

organized like an army. There were about thirty thousand stationed throughout Spain—well-armed and well-trained. The peasants and workers had hated them for years for their alleged brutality.

In Castilblanco the fate of the *Guardia Civil* was terrible. When they tried to break up the Anarchist meeting the entire population of the village fell upon them. They were all killed and their bodies were horribly mutilated. On one of the bodies thirty-seven knife wounds were found.

But dissatisfaction with the Republican government was not confined to peasants, separatists, and the Church. As the government in Madrid made a beginning towards dismantling the top-heavy military structure that had burdened the state for so many years, the Army officers decided to act. Making an agreement with Monarchists and the Church to restore Alfonso XIII to the throne, they found a leader in General José Sanjurjo. Arms were distributed, and in August of 1932, the Army seized control of Seville and tried to take over Madrid itself. But the government had heard of their plans and was prepared for them. The rebellion was quickly crushed and its leaders imprisoned. The organizers of the conspiracy lived to act another day.

Aware that he lacked support from important segments of the nation, Prime Minister Manuel Azaña resigned, and new general elections were called for November 19, 1933. Now the foolishness of extending the vote to Spain's barely literate and Church-dominated women became apparent. In the new *Cortes* the rightists, including Catholic, Monarchist, and ultra-conservative groups, gained 207 seats; the middle-of-the-road center parties won 167 seats; and the leftists won only 99. It was a clear-cut victory for the conservative, not to say reactionary, elements in Spanish life. With Alcalá Zamora still President, a new Prime Minister, the conservative Alejandro Lerroux, proceeded to rescind many of the former government's reforms—especially

José Antonio

those dealing with the disestablishment of the Catholic Church.

It was in this atmosphere of reaction that José Antonio Primo de Rivera founded a new political party called the *Falange* in 1933. José Antonio was the son of the old dictator Primo de Rivera, and much of his life and work can be seen as an attempt to vindicate his father's memory. He was a tall, handsome young man with admitted courage and charm—and an abiding distrust of democratic forms. He had begun his career as a Monarchist, and although always a devout Catholic personally, he distrusted Church influence in government. Now that conservative reaction seemed to be in the ascendancy in Spain, José Antonio gathered around himself a group of students, lawyers, small shopkeepers, younger Army officers, and ex-Socialists, all of whom shared a deep dislike of the democratic process. They chose the name

Falange for their new party because that had been the name of the
Macedonian battle units that destroyed democracy in ancient
Greece. The *Falange* symbols were a yoke and a sheaf of arrows.
The *Falange* philosophy was Fascist. But fascism, which is anti-
intellectual, is not so much a system of thought, not so much a
definable political position as it is an emotional disease. It has
been different in each country. It is marked by fear, basically—
the fear that breeds hatred and intolerance of whatever is different,
whatever does not conform to the simplest patterns of behavior,
whatever cannot be directly and completely *controlled*. Frightened
by the problems and complexities of modern life, Fascists seek to
simplify through destruction and control through force. Fascism
is a psychological condition that can be found among people of all
countries, including our own. The *Falange* program in Spain had
some similarities to and certain differences from the programs of
Mussolini in Italy and Hitler in Germany. There was the same desire to control thought, the same determination to do away with
such organizations as trade unions that might act independently
of the state, the same desire to seize and control the nation's industries, the same program of abolition of politics and absolute
control of the government by a single party. On the other hand,
although it criticized the Church for being an ally of monarchy,
the *Falange,* far from being antireligious like the Nazis, made the
Catholic traditions of Spain the center of its social ideals. And,
although fiercely proud of their heritage, the Falangists never developed Hitlerian racial hatreds. The *Falange* did not attract much
support among the masses of Spain. But it organized its younger
members into military groups, armed and trained them, and em-
barked upon a policy of street warfare and political murder.

As the conservative government in Madrid proceeded with the
dismantling of many Republican reforms, it soon became apparent
that the real power in Madrid was held by the solid bloc of rightist
parties led by José María Gil Robles—a politician notorious for

his anti-democratic views. Discontent was widespread among peasants, workers, and separatists, all of whom felt betrayed, when, in October, 1934, a new series of appointments to the Cabinet brought Gil Robles himself into the government. It was the signal for an avalanche.

Within days of the new Cabinet appointments a general strike paralyzed the entire country, while in Barcelona the Catalans proclaimed themselves an independent state within a Spanish Federal Republic. The Catalan uprising was speedily put down by the Spanish Army, happy to cooperate with a government that was Republican in name only, but a far more serious threat was posed by events in Asturias.

In that same October of 1934, disgusted by the reactionary policies of the Robles-dominated government in Madrid and certain now that the conservative politicians in their nation's capital were preparing to turn over power to Monarchists and Fascists (as conservatives had in Germany, Italy, and Austria), the Socialist miners of Asturias in the far north of Spain united to set up a separate government, organized loosely on the Soviet model. These miners were tough, well-educated politically, highly organized, and they had arms and plenty of dynamite. They quickly seized control of the province, killing most of the *Guardia Civil* in their region and taking over churches, town halls, and other important buildings. Within ten days they had set up a radio station at Turón, taken over the large arms factories in Trubía and Oviedo, and mobilized thirty thousand workers into a "Red Army." While their militia forced the Regular Army units in Asturias to hole up near Avila, the miners' committee planned a march on Madrid and proclaimed a Socialist Republic for all of Spain.

The conservative government in Madrid, faced by what was clearly a major uprising, called once again upon the Army for help. They brought units of the Foreign Legion over from

General Franco

Morocco and gave command of the operation to General Francisco Franco, one of the Legion's former commanders. These tough professional soldiers were immediately successful. They were supported by some native Moroccan troops and by aircraft. Brushing aside the miners' militia, they quickly reconquered the entire province. But what followed was terrible. Over a thousand civilians were shot without trial by the legionnaires and thirty thousand thrown into prisons, where many were tortured to death. Luis Sirval, a journalist who reported these terrible events, was himself arrested and murdered in prison by three young officers of the Legion. But in Madrid General Franco and his men were called saviors of the nation— by the conservative government.

By the beginning of 1936, the paralysis of Spanish government was almost complete. The conservative majority in the *Cortes,* determined either to undo or at least to stifle the Republican reforms, had run head-on into the violent opposition of the masses of workers and peasants throughout the country. Unfortunately, many of these tended to blame the Republican government as such, as well as the rightist parties, for their continuing misery. In any event, President Alcalá Zamora exercised his authority to dissolve the *Cortes* and call for new general elections, which were held on February 16, 1936.

To oppose the rightist parties clustered around the leadership of Gil Robles, the Socialists, Liberals, and Republicans united in one large Popular Front group for the elections of 1936. After a bitterly fought campaign, their tactics were rewarded by a huge victory. The new *Cortes*—the last freely elected *Cortes* in Spanish history thus far—was to be composed of 256 leftists, 165 rightists, and 52 centrists. Thus the Socialist-Republican bloc commanded an absolute majority in the government.

Once again Manuel Azaña became Prime Minister and organized a cabinet of leftist politicians. However, continued violence in the countryside and the continued obstructionism of Gil Robles' followers in the new *Cortes* soon forced a governmental shake-up. Alcalá Zamora was replaced as President by Manuel Azaña, and Santiago Casares Quiroga was named Prime Minister. But the problems that beset Spain were now almost beyond the hope of democratic solutions. Anarchists and certain extremist Socialists predicted a revolution from the left, while Falangists, Monarchists, and the Army plotted to seize power from the right. A meeting of the *Cortes* on June 16, 1936, made it clear to all who could understand that things would not continue as they had.

Calvo Sotelo, a former Monarchist who had once been Finance Minister in the government of the old dictator Primo de Rivera, arose to declare, "Against this sterile state I am proposing the integrated state. . . . (such a) state many may call Fascist; if this indeed be the Fascist state, then I, who believe in it, proudly declare myself a Fascist!"

One of the handful of Communists in the *Cortes* answered Sotelo. She was a handsome woman of fierce temperament—her name, Dolores Ibarruri, better known to Spain and to history as *La Pasionaria*. She had once been a devout Catholic, making a living selling sardines to poor Basque villagers. But she married a Communist miner from Asturias and adopted her husband's politics with the same fanaticism she had once brought to her religion. She declared that day in the *Cortes* that, although Spanish Fascists were merely gangsters, Spain might fall victim to an international Fascist conspiracy directed from Rome and Berlin.

Gil Robles made the day's most prophetic statement. "A country," he declared, "can live under a monarchy or a republic, with a parliamentary or a presidential system, under communism or fascism! But it cannot live in anarchy. Now, alas, Spain is in anarchy. And we are present today at the funeral service of democracy!"

Casares Quiroga, the liberal Prime Minister, attempted to answer this by crying, "I give my assurance, Parliament will work and the Army will do its duty!"

But who in that crowded chamber, amid the jeers and cheers, the insults and the flaming oratory, believed him? Now events rushed towards their tragic climax.

The higher Army officers, led by Generals Franco and Sanjurjo, made an agreement with the Monarchists, José Antonio's *Falange,* many of the Catholic conservatives, and some of the nation's richest businessmen to lead the Army in sudden rebellion against the Republic and seize power. And although the vaguely suspicious government of the Republic arrested and imprisoned José Antonio in Alicante while sending General Franco to the Canary Islands far out in the Atlantic, their plans ripened.

The chaotic conditions in Spain on the brink of civil war are perfectly illustrated by two murders that took place on the very eve of the Army's uprising. At nine o'clock in the evening of July

12, 1936, Lieutenant José Castillo of the Republican security police was walking home after his day's work in Madrid. Just a few months before, in the line of duty, he had shot and killed a cousin of José Antonio during a riot. Since that day his life had been threatened time and again by the *Falange* street fighters. When he married in June, his new bride received an anonymous letter demanding to know why she married a man who would be so soon a corpse. As Lieutenant Castillo reached his home on that sultry summer evening, he was shot and killed by four men with pistols who quickly escaped. When the news of this murder reached Republican security police headquarters, Lieutenant Castillo's former comrades became enraged. Some suggested that they should immediately rush out into the streets and shoot it out with any *Falange* street gangs they could find. But finally it was decided to take vengeance not on the *Falange* gunmen who had committed the crime but on a prominent right-wing political leader.

Very early on the morning of July 13, a car left security police

". . . unless these gentlemen intend to blow out my brains."
The body of Calvo Sotelo, recovered from the East Cemetery in
Madrid, July 14, 1936.

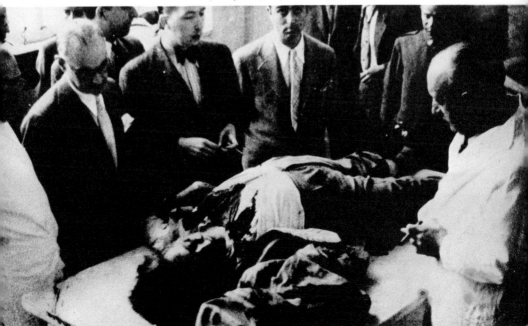

headquarters and raced through the empty streets of the capital. In it were several well-armed policemen. Their objective was the home of Calvo Sotelo, one of the political leaders of Spain's right-wing parties. When they appeared at the door of his apartment, Sotelo inspected their credentials. They told him he was wanted on urgent police matters at headquarters. He agreed to go with them and told his anxious family he would telephone as soon as he found out what was wanted of him. "That is," he added, "unless these gentlemen intend to blow out my brains." So the police car, with Calvo Sotelo in it, raced off at eighty miles an hour into the night. No one spoke. After the car had gone a few blocks, one of the policemen sitting behind Sotelo pulled out a revolver and shot him twice through the back of the neck. The body was delivered as that of some unknown vagabond to the East Cemetery in Madrid. It was not identified and removed until the following day.

Now the right-wing parties formally withdrew from the *Cortes*. It was plain, they said, that the Republican government could not even control its own police force. The Socialist and Anarchist labor unions, alarmed by this, armed their members with what few weapons they could find and waited to see what would happen. Isolated shootings took place in Madrid, politicians made their usual inflammatory statements, and the government hesitated to bring the murderers of Calvo Sotelo to trial. A riot in which several people were killed took place when the funeral parties of Lieutenant Castillo and Calvo Sotelo accidentally met at the Madrid Cemetery. All through the terrible heat of the July day following these senseless murders, Spain waited in an agony of fear. Would it be civil war?

Only a very small group of generals, Monarchists, and Falangists knew that the first act of the great Civil War drama had, in fact, already started. They were awaiting the arrival in the Canary Islands of a French aircraft piloted by an Englishman to unleash the great battle.

II

Rebellion
and
Revolution

On July 11, 1936—just one day before Lieutenant Castillo's murder in Madrid—a French airplane of the type known as a *Dragon Rapide* taxied down the long runway of Croydon Airport outside London. At the controls sat an English pilot, Captain Bebb. Captain Bebb knew his destination but not much else about the trip. His passengers were Luis Bolin, the London correspondent of Madrid's Monarchist newspaper, *ABC,* and several English ladies and gentlemen—none of whom knew the purpose of their journey. They had all been procured by Douglas Jerrold, an English publisher who had managed to keep his motives secret. As the *Dragon Rapide* lifted off the runway and wheeled south through the misty English sky, no one aboard knew he was the final link in an intricate conspiracy.

For the bargainings and plottings of the generals, the Monarchists, and the Falangists in Spain had now ripened and borne fruit. Under the leadership of Generals José Sanjurjo, Manuel Goded, Emilio Mola, and Francisco Franco, they had completed plans for a rebellion of Army garrisons throughout the country that would topple the Republican government. While they were not quite agreed as to what was to replace it, they were united in their hatred of what they considered the weak and anarchic regime in Madrid. But for their plans to be effective it was essential that the Army of Africa, composed of the Spanish Foreign Legion and native Moroccan troops, rebel, cross the Straits of Gibraltar, and aid the uprisings on the mainland. And if there was one man in Spain who could assure the support of the Army of Africa it was General Francisco Franco, one of its former commanders. But General Franco had been sent by the nervous Republican government to a remote command on one of the Canary Islands, far out in the Atlantic. Thus the necessity for the *Dragon Rapide*—a plane faster than any at the disposal of the plotters in Spain—and of Captain Bebb, whom the plotters considered more reliable than any of their own pilots. The passengers were merely window dressing to disguise the purpose of the trip. Colonel Alfredo Kindelán of the Spanish Air Force, one of the conspirators, had instructed Torcuato Luca de Tena, editor of *ABC*, to hire the plane. De Tena in turn had ordered Luis Bolín to arrange matters. The plane was to proceed to Lisbon, refuel, and then fly directly to Las Palmas Airport in the Canary Islands. There it would take aboard General Franco and transport him to Morocco.

General Francisco Franco y Bahamonde (the last name, as is customary in Spain, being that of his mother's family) was just forty-four at this time. He was born in El Ferrol, a port city of the province of Galicia, into a family whose members traditionally entered the Navy. But, in the year that young Francisco Franco applied for entry, there was no room for him in the Naval Cadet School. So instead, in 1907, he entered the Infantry Academy in Toledo. After his training he was sent to Morocco where the Spanish were fighting a desperate war against the fierce Riff tribesmen to maintain control of their African colony. Franco, demonstrating tremendous personal courage in battle, a keen eye for organizational details, and a genuine ability to understand and deal with the local Moorish chieftains, quickly rose to become the youngest general in the Spanish Army. He commanded the Foreign Legion for four years, reorganizing it and winning its loyalty. It was his plan of landing from the sea behind the Riff lines that eventually brought about the Spanish victory.

General Franco was short, balding, and given to plumpness; his voice was high-pitched. But during those years of battle he earned the complete respect and devotion of the tough professional soldiers of the Foreign Legion and the loyalty even of the native Moorish troops. He was completely dedicated to the Army, known as a strict disciplinarian and a man of extremely conservative personal habits. He never drank, rarely went out with women, and during his earlier years seemed indifferent to the Church. Later, after his marriage to Carmen Polo, a strongly Catholic girl of good Asturian family, religion was to become important to him.

During the years of the Republic Franco had a reputation as the "brilliant young general" in Madrid. But, with a caution that was unusual in Spain but was to stand him in good stead over the years, he refused to become involved in the chaotic political machinations of the various parties. The Monarchists could not claim him, nor could the Republicans. He was certainly not a

Socialist, nor was he a Falangist. The rightist government of 1934 trusted him enough to give him command of the forces that crushed the miners' revolt in Asturias.

But if he refused to commit himself, General Franco was very well-read politically. He was drawn to the right wing of Spanish politics by the naturally conservative heritage of army life, by his belief in the older traditions of Catholic Spain, and by his disgust with the anarchy into which the country seemed to be drifting. The election of February 16, 1936, with the victory of a completely left-wing government, was apparently the factor deciding him to throw in his lot with the conspirators. When this new government sent him to the Canary Islands, he warned of the danger of anarchy. His warnings were dismissed. A few months later, on the eve of his rebellion, Franco wrote again to the Madrid government, protesting against its removal of right-wing Army officers from certain posts. He warned that such procedures threatened to undermine the Army's morale and discipline. No reply was ever received to this letter.

But by that time it was too late. As the *Dragon Rapide* reached Lisbon, the body of Calvo Sotelo was being buried in Madrid. And as Captain Bebb and his airplane landed at Las Palmas in the Canary Islands, rioting gripped the Spanish capital. Captain Bebb made up endlessly ingenious stories for the local airport authorities at Las Palmas as to why he had landed there without papers. But he had not long to wait for his passengers. For, in the early morning hours of July 17, General Franco, accompanied by his wife and small daughter, arrived at Las Palmas from a neighboring island. The General planned to wait a few days and then announce the rebellion. But matters were taken out of his hands.

For, as General Franco arrived at Las Palmas, the first sparks of rebellion had been ignited accidentally in distant Morocco. There, on the morning of July 18, 1936, certain Spanish Army officers were completing the details of their plot to seize control of the city of Melilla on Morocco's Mediterranean coast. Colonel Almuzara Seguí, their leader, now felt free to inform his civilian allies of the local *Falange* of the exact hour of the rebellion: five o'clock. But among the Falangists was a spy who immediately informed General Quintero Romerales, the Republic's *Comandante* in the city, of what was afoot. Romerales was one of the fattest of Spain's generals, and one of the most easygoing and foolish. When he learned that the conspirators had armed themselves and were meeting in the Map Department of Army Headquarters, he sent a Lieutenant Juan Zaro in charge of a handful of police and troops to surround the building, search for arms, and arrest the plotters. Finding themselves discovered and besieged within the headquarters building, the conspirators telephoned to a Foreign Legion unit to rescue them. When these troops arrived, Lieutenant Zaro felt he could not open fire on them. He quietly surrendered. Colonel Seguí went immediately to General Romerales' office. There, with a pistol in his hand, he forced the indecisive general to resign. The rebel officers then declared a state of war, occupied all official and key communications buildings in the city, closed down all trade union and left-wing political headquarters, and arrested all Republican leaders. There was a violent but short struggle in the working-class districts of the city, but as the workers were taken by surprise and unarmed, they were overwhelmed. By evening the city was conquered, and all those who had resisted the rebels, including General Romerales, were shot. Meantime, forced to act prematurely, Colonel Seguí had sent out the telegraph signal that was the code word for risings to begin all over Spain: "sin novedades" (without news).

Receiving this signal in the Canary Islands, General Franco ordered out the Army garrisons, made himself master of the Islands (though final resistance was not crushed for several days) and declared martial law. On the morning of July 18, he broadcast a manifesto to the nation in which he appealed to Army officers to place loyalty to country above loyalty to the present Republican government, join the uprising, and help build a new order that victory had been won. Then, on July 19, he boarded the *Dragon Rapide* and took off for Tetuán in Morocco, with Captain Bebb still at the controls. He was eagerly awaited.

Resistance in the other principal cities of Morocco had been brief and ineffective, though at times bloody. In Tetuán and Ceuta, rebel officers seized control almost without a fight. In Larache, on the Atlantic coast, there was bitter fighting in working-class districts. But it was all over by dawn of July 18. The local Moorish chieftains also announced their support of the rebellion. Henceforth the rebels could count not only on the tough Army of Africa but also on a secure base in North Africa.

What was the reaction of the government to these events? At first it apparently believed it was faced only by a colonial uprising. Three destroyers were dispatched to Melilla to support General Romerales, and when they arrived too late, a few planes were sent to bomb the rebel-held city. Generals Franco, Goded, Mola, and Sanjurjo were dismissed from the Army and declared traitors. The Liberal Prime Minister, Casares Quiroga, was constantly telephoning to loyalists in Morocco urging them not to give up the struggle. These half-measures were, of course, useless. And as news of the rebellion spread (in spite of the government's silence), left-wing political parties and trade union leaders in Madrid, anticipating risings now throughout the Spanish mainland, demanded that the government issue arms to the workers. In reply, Casares Quiroga announced that anyone arming the masses would be shot. He and his Liberal government feared that once weapons found their way into the hands of peasants and workers, Spain would be swept by a left-wing revolution. Mobs were already forming in Madrid. But while the people listened sceptically to the government's radio announcement that "no

Queipo de Llano

one, absolutely no one on the Spanish mainland, has taken part in this absurd plot," rebellion had, in fact, already broken out in the cities of Andalusia.

Everywhere in the southern cities of Spain the pattern was the same. Led by their officers, the local Army garrison would seize control of the city. Then the rebel leader would proclaim a state of war, force the civil governor to resign, and attempt to arrest the Republican leaders. The workers and peasants, led by their trade union and political leaders, would call a general strike, erect barricades, and resist the rebel troops and their Falangist allies with whatever weapons they could find. The fighting was always fierce, passionate, and ruthless in the working-class districts.

The great Andalusian city of Seville witnessed an amazing bluff by the rebel General Queipo de Llano. He was one of the arch-conspirators, and the conquest of Seville had been his assignment, even though he knew little of the city. But Queipo de Llano was nothing if not bold. He arrived in the city on the morning of July 17, in an automobile, accompanied only by his aide and three other officers. Finding that the headquarters building was empty because of the excessive heat, Queipo took over one of the offices. Then he walked down the deserted corridors of the building until he found General Villa-Abraille, *Comandante* of the Seville garrison.

"I must tell you," Queipo announced to the General and his staff, "that the time has come to make a decision. Either you are with me and your brother officers, or you are with this government which is leading Spain to ruin."

Villa-Abraille and his staff were afraid to commit themselves. They knew that if the rebellion failed they faced the death of traitors. Queipo arrested them and ordered them into the next room. Since that room had no key, he simply stationed a corporal outside the door and ordered him to shoot anyone who tried to emerge. Then, accompanied only by his aide, he went over to the infantry barracks. There, to his surprise, he found the regiment drawn up under arms in the compound. Walking up to the regimental colonel, whom he had never seen before, Queipo said, "I shake your hand, my dear Colonel, and congratulate you for deciding to put yourself on the side of your brothers-in-arms!"

But the colonel eyed him coldly and replied, "I have decided to support the government!"

Unshaken, Queipo simply said, "Shall we continue this interview in your office?"

But although he accompanied Queipo to his office, the colonel refused to change his mind. So Queipo coolly dismissed him from command of the regiment. But then he could find no one else to take command. All the regimental officers were afraid that the conspiracy might fail. Finally he found a captain to take charge. Then, striding to the back of the room, Queipo shouted, "You are all my prisoners!" The regimental officers thereupon allowed themselves to be arrested. Next Queipo discovered that there were only one hundred and thirty men in this "regiment." A handful of armed civilian Falangists had by now joined him; but how could he expect, with these tiny forces, to conquer a city of a quarter of a million people?

The turning point came when Queipo persuaded an artillery battery to join him. Heavy guns were wheeled into the city, and the offices of the civil governor were surrounded. The governor then telephoned to surrender himself on condition that his life be spared.

But while Queipo slowly took over the center of the city, the working-class districts learned what was happening. Huge crowds milled around the trade union headquarters demanding arms. Radio Seville called for a general strike and begged the peasants in neighboring villages to rush to help their comrades in the city. Churches were set afire, and barricades appeared everywhere on the streets.

In the evening, Queipo captured the radio station and personally broadcast that Spain was saved and that the "rabble" who resisted would be shot like dogs. By nightfall Seville was divided into two armed camps. It was only with the arrival of Moorish troops some days later that the workers' resistance was finally drowned in blood and the city lost to the Republic.

Almost everywhere in Andalusia on that hot July day, the rebellion was successful. Cadiz, Jerez, Algeciras, La Línea—all fell into rebel hands. But in Granada the conspirators were afraid to act because of vast popular demonstrations and the Republican sympathies of the commanding general. In Málaga the rebel generals surrendered when they were threatened by a bombardment from the Republican warships lying in the harbor. But these isolated successes only underscored the fact that much of southern Spain was now in rebel hands.

Meanwhile, the government of Casares Quiroga in Madrid continued to hesitate. Government officers talked endlessly and passed their time discussing possible compromises, none of which were to prove acceptable to the rebels. They continued to issue misleading statements, but they could not for long hide the truth from the people. Ordinary workers learned what was happening in Andalusia by the simple expedient of telephoning their friends in the various cities and towns. The Spanish telephone service was managed by an American company, and it continued to serve both sides impartially throughout the Civil War. The French writer André Malraux has described how these telephone calls often went:

Madrid: "Hello, Avila—how is everything down there? This is the railroad station."

Avila: "We'll show you, dirty pig! Long live Christ the King!"

Madrid: "See you soon, good health!"

A delegation of drivers offered the government three thousand taxis to fight the rebels. A Socialist trade union distributed eight thousand rifles to its youth organization. Special editions of the newspapers demanded "Arms for the People!" in huge headlines. Mobs began to form in the streets. But still the government refused to hand out arms.

The crowds that had been filling Madrid's streets all that hot July 17 now converged at the Puerta del Sol. Government loudspeakers had been rigged up and between bursts of martial music they would announce: "People of Spain! Keep tuned in. Do not turn your radios off. Rumors are being circulated by traitors. Keep tuned in!" That evening, for the first time, the people of Spain heard the compelling voice of *La Pasionaria* over Radio Madrid. She demanded arms for the workers, urged women to fight with knives and burning oil, and cried, "It is better to die on your feet than to live on your knees! No pasarán!" This slogan —"No pasarán!" (they shall not pass, the battle cry of the French at Verdun during the First World War)—was to become the battle cry of the Republic.

"La Pasionaria"

The government of Casares Quiroga, which had vacillated all day, had now become an object of deep suspicion to a majority of the people. The crowds in the Puerta del Sol were chanting, "Treason! Traitors!" and "Arms, arms, arms!" President Manuel Azaña, conscious of the possible consequences of arming the people, was nevertheless convinced that only the workers and peasants could now save the Republic. Therefore, during the night of July 18, he called in the Socialist leaders Indalecio Prieto and Largo Caballero. They agreed with him that arms must be distributed at once and agreed also to give their full support to a new government of Liberals. The Anarchists and Communists also agreed to support a new government. Neither of these parties would take an actual part in governing—that would be associating themselves with middle-class rule—but they agreed in the emergency to back a Liberal regime in hope of rallying at least a part of Spain's small middle classes to the side of the workers. José Giral, a former professor of chemistry, was named Prime Minister. Radio Madrid announced that the new government was ready to reply to "fascism's declaration of war on the Spanish people."

Giral immediately ordered arms to be given to the crowds. At dawn on July 19, trucks full of rifles roared through the streets of Madrid to trade union headquarters, where, amid scenes of great jubilation, arms were distributed to the people. At the same time, Giral ordered the civil governors of the various provinces to distribute guns to the workers and peasants. His action came just in time—for on July 19 the second great shock of rebellion erupted throughout the nation.

The rebel generals were not to be so successful on July 18 in the north of Spain as they had been in the south the day before. There were several reasons for this. First of all, the people had been warned by the previous day's risings in Andalusia; secondly, they were now armed by order of the government; thirdly, the industrialized workers of the north were better educated politically than the essentially agricultural people of the south; and finally, in the north the rebel generals had to fight not only against Republican sentiment but also against the home rule movements in Catalonia and the Basque country.

Luis Companys, President of the locally autonomous Catalan government, at first, like Quiroga in Madrid, refused to issue arms to the people of Barcelona, Catalonia's great port and capital. Like Quiroga, too, he feared a left-wing revolution in the city. But here the highly organized trade unions simply stormed several of the city's principal arsenals and issued guns on their own authority.

General Francisco Llano de la Encomienda, *Comandante* of the division of the Regular Army based at Barcelona, was not a member of the generals' conspiracy. He went so far as to warn his fellow officers that if they acted in such a way as to force him to make a choice between fascism and communism, he would without hesitation choose communism. When President Companys telephoned Encomienda on July 18 to ask how things were with the garrison, the General assured him that everything was normal.

But among Encomienda's officers the plot was well advanced. The leader of the rebels in Barcelona was General Fernández Burriel—but final command was reserved for General Manuel Goded, one of the four chiefs of the conspiracy, who was to fly in from the Balearic Islands (after seizing them), just as Franco was arriving in Morocco from the Canaries.

Burriel's plan was very simple. The troops of various barracks throughout the city would be called out and they would converge at the Plaza de Cataluña, Barcelona's principal square. Burriel assumed he would have no difficulty in taking over the city. But he had not reckoned with two vital factors—the arming of the people and the *Guardia Civil*. For in Barcelona, unlike most of the rest of Spain, the well-armed and well-trained *Guardia Civil* was staunchly Republican.

The hot dawn of July 19 found the streets of Barcelona filled with armed workers. Radio Madrid's passionate appeals to the people bawled from public loudspeakers. A mounted troop of *Guardia Civil,* trotting down the Ramblas (Barcelona's main boulevard) gave the clenched-fist Communist salute while the crowds cheered enthusiastically.

Meanwhile the rebel officers had called out the Army garrison. It may be asked why here, as elsewhere in Spain, the soldiers, who were mostly from worker or peasant families, agreed to rise on behalf of the rebels? The fact is that apart from the deep-rooted sense of obedience and discipline which any army impresses upon its rank and file, and apart from the volunteer soldiers who were quite willing to fight anyone at all, most of Spain's conscript army was composed of nearly illiterate young men. They, amid the frantic political confusion of the times, simply could not understand what was at stake. The only certainty in their lives was what their officers ordered them to do. Even so, very many units refused to follow orders. The fleet, for example, composed of better-educated specialists, gave its officers a bloody surprise. And many garrisons were fooled by their officers. This is what happened in Barcelona. One barracks was told that it was being called out to put down an Anarchist revolution; another was told it was to parade through the town. Of course, once a soldier was faced by armed enemies firing upon him, the question of why or how he had got there became academic. He fought to save his own life.

But when the various columns that were to meet at the Plaza de Cataluña marched into the streets, they found themselves immediately confronted by thousands upon thousands of armed and desperate workers. Fierce battles broke out everywhere. Only one small battery of artillery was able to reach the Plaza. The soldiers seized control of the telephone exchange, but instantly found themselves besieged within it. Everywhere throughout the city, rebel commanders found themselves baffled by the revolutionary tactics of the armed masses. One column of troops was met by armed workers who, with rifles held aloft, simply pleaded and argued with the soldiers until they finally turned and shot down their officers and then joined the people. But most of the battles were fierce. The soldiers were only overcome by heroic sacrifices on the part of the masses. One rebel machine gun was silenced, for example, by an unknown factory worker who simply threw himself onto its spitting barrel. At midday General Goded arrived from the Balearics—but it was too late. By evening it was all over. Goded broadcast an appeal to his men to surrender and was himself arrested along with other rebels. Barcelona had been saved for the Republic.

With certain exceptions the story was the same throughout the

North. In Asturias, whose miners had so recently revolted against the former rightist government, a clever rebel officer, Colonel Antonio Aranda, tricked the Republicans into believing he was loyal, thereby seizing the city of Oviedo. But the miners, armed with and expert in the use of dynamite, soon flocked into the city from the surrounding countryside and besieged the Colonel and his men. Most of the rest of Asturias was quickly secured for the Republic, and a large trainload of armed and enthusiastic miners was dispatched to Madrid to help the people of the capital.

In the fiercely independent Basque country the rebels enjoyed few victories. In the great industrial port city of Bilbao the rebels never even left their barracks. In San Sebastián on the French border, Spain's summer capital, the rebels delayed action until it was too late. They found themselves besieged in the María Cristina Hotel by hordes of armed workers. Throughout the Basque region, councils of defense were immediately set up by the workers; right-wing politicians, the rich, and the suspect were quickly arrested, and the industry of the country was mobilized for war.

The heavily conservative provinces of Spain—Old Castile, Aragon, and Navarre—showed greater rebel success on July 19. The ancient cities of Burgos, Saragossa, Pamplona, and Valladolid all fell to the rebels—often without a struggle, for the populations were strongly Monarchist. In Valladolid, General Lobero Molero, *Comandante* of the garrison, was not part of the conspiracy. He was greatly surprised therefore at noon when two rebel generals appeared in his office and demanded that he declare himself for the uprising. They gave him fifteen minutes in his inner office in which to make up his mind. While the minutes passed gunfire could be heard in the streets as Falangists and workers started shooting it out. Suddenly General Molero burst from the inner office shouting, "Viva la República!" A short pistol battle followed but soon ended with Molero under arrest. He was led away, and later shot.

In the province of Galicia, on the Atlantic coast, the port cities of El Ferrol, Corunna, and Vigo were seized by the rebels early in the day. But the crews of the warships in the harbors were strongly Republican and opened fire on the rebel-held towns. The battleship *España* and her sister ships continued to lob heavy shells into the city of El Ferrol all through the night. The crews had overpowered their officers, some being shot, most imprisoned.

Practically everywhere in the fleet the story was the same. The officers were either part of the conspiracy or tried to join it. The crews, when they found out what was happening, would refuse to obey orders, arrest the officers, and usually execute them. The cruisers *Cervantes* and *Libertad* and the battleship *Jaime Primero* had been ordered from their home ports to Morocco to help put down the rebellion there. But the officers had other ideas. When the seamen saw that their officers intended to sabotage the government's orders, they mutinied. Urged on by messages from the Admiralty in Madrid which were addressed to the crews rather than the commanders, the sailors shot it out with their officers. On the *Jaime Primero* the officers resisted to the last man. When the crew radioed Madrid asking what to do with their bodies, they were instructed to "lower bodies overboard with respectful solemnity." By nightfall of July 19, the fleet was almost entirely in Republican hands. With the ships run by committees of sailors, the fleet gathered in the Straits of Gibraltar to prevent General Franco from transporting the Army of Africa to the mainland. But already a few units of legionnaires and Moroccans had reached Algeciras. Their presence was to prove decisive in many of the cities of Andalusia. Certain stalemates were now being broken in that region.

In the city of Granada the mutual stand-off between the Republican crowds in the streets and Falangists was brought to an end when rebel Army units at last sallied forth from their barracks to disperse the unarmed workers. But though they conquered the center of the city without a shot, it was not until after a battle of near-extermination had been fought out in the workers' quarter of the city that Granada became secure for the rebels.

On the other hand, farther north, in the great port cities of Valencia and Alicante, events took a different turn. There, after some indecision, loyal Republican officers and certain units of the *Guardia Civil* along with armed workers easily took control.

It was only now, on July 20, that the uprising in Madrid took place. But the rebels had waited too long. By the time they acted, the trade unions were ready for them. The rebels, under General Juaquín Fanjul, attempted to sally forth from the Montaña Barracks in the city. They were prevented by a huge mob of people so dense they literally could not cut their way through. These people brandished rifles—but the bolts for the rifles were inside the Montaña Barracks. The rebels found themselves under siege in the barracks—as indeed they were in barracks and Army posts throughout the city. Two artillery pieces (drawn up by a beer truck) opened fire on the Montaña Barracks about noon. Soon a white flag appeared at one of the windows. But when the crowd surged forward to enter, machine guns opened up on them. Twice more white flags appeared; twice more, when the people tried to accept the surrender, they were cut down by machine gun fire. The mob became maddened. They burst into the barracks and massacred all whom they found alive. Officers were shot on sight— some were thrown from the windows onto the heads of the enraged mob below. A very few were rushed off to imprisonment in Madrid's Model Prison. The fate of the other barracks was similar. On the airfields around Madrid Republican officers prevented the rebels from taking any action, while in the artillery barracks at Carabanchel the rebel general was killed by his own men.

The armed workers, jubilant over the success in Madrid, now sent columns to the neighboring cities of Toledo and Guadalajara.

Colonel Moscardó

There the rebellion had been successful, but both cities were quickly recaptured for the Republic. In Toledo, the rebel Colonel Moscardó retreated with 1,300 men, their wives and children, and about 100 Republican hostages, into a strong fortress known as the Alcázar. There, well-armed but with little food, he prepared to hold out in a siege that was to become legendary throughout the world.

Thus, by July 21, the battle lines were fairly well-defined in Spain. The center of the country and the entire eastern seaboard, including the cities of Madrid, Barcelona, Valencia, Alicante, and all the surrounding provinces, were firmly held by the Republic. In the north, Asturias and the entire Basque region were likewise in Republican hands. But between Madrid and the Basques was a large area, including the provinces of Old Castile, Navarre, and Aragon, as well as the seacoast province of Galicia, that was firmly rebel. The rebels held the cities of Cadiz, Burgos, Granada, Seville, and Algeciras, as well as the port cities of El Ferrol and Vigo. In Andalusia the rebels held most of the towns, but the surrounding countryside was still in the hands of the Republican peasants. In some cities rebels held individual buildings while the Republicans held the rest of the town, while in others the situation was reversed. Only in Morocco had the rebels been everywhere completely victorious. There, General Franco arrived in his *Dragon Rapide* in the forenoon of July 19. He had at his command the battle-tested and professional Army of Africa—but he faced the problem of transporting this force to the mainland against the Republican fleet and air forces.

These opening days of rebellion witnessed what Casares Quiroga had feared: revolution throughout Republican Spain. The armed masses, seeing that the forces of law and order, the Army and the *Guardia Civil,* were mostly on the side of the rebels, took the law into their own hands. Old grudges and ancient hatreds were settled with bullets. In the villages, towns, and smaller cities, councils of workers and peasants, sometimes organized by the Socialists, sometimes by the Anarchists, appointed themselves as the government. They passed laws, seized the property of the rich, and arrested and executed whatever rebels fell into their hands. The Basques finally set up a completely autonomous republic of their own, while in Catalonia the autonomous government of Luis Companys was now independent in everything but name. Spain had dissolved; and its reunification presented as great a problem to the Republican government of Madrid as did the Civil War.

In the great wave of violence that broke over the country, atrocities were committed by both sides. In many Republican districts the churches were burned, convents pillaged, priests and sometimes nuns executed—often with great cruelty. The rich, the upper middle classes, and the aristocrats suffered loss of their possessions and, very often, execution. It has been estimated that

Luis Companys

75,000 civilians lost their lives to trigger-happy Republican militiamen or were executed after the flimsiest of trials during the Civil War. But this was not the government's policy. The common people of Spain could not be controlled as they avenged the grievances of a thousand years, blindly and savagely, upon their nearest enemies.

In the areas held by the rebels, things were not much better. Workers and peasants were massacred wholesale when villages and cities were conquered by rebel troops. Republican politicians, trade union officials—all suspected of loyalty to the Republic were executed, often without trial. It is believed that 40,000 people fell victim to rebel "justice" during the Civil War. Of course many of the worst atrocities were committed by battle-crazed troops immediately after the conquest of a village or town. But a certain amount of terrorism, directed against intellectuals and leaders, appeared to be part of the policy of the rebel authorities who felt themselves everywhere in the minority.

All over Spain, on both sides, lawless cruelty and violence had its day. Peasants shot down priests who were in the act of blessing them, aristocrats tortured illiterate workers to death, workers massacred Army officers, even when they protested that they were Republicans. And, as in every war, both sides felt they were committing these atrocious deeds for the noblest of causes. By the time some sort of order had been established on each side of the battle lines, hatreds had been aroused that only blood could wipe out. On both sides, Republican and Nationalist (as the rebels soon called themselves), Spaniards went to war joyfully, ferociously. It was very soon apparent that the war would be long, bitter, and merciless, and that a night of agony had settled over Spain.

III

The World Takes Sides

THE clash of political ideas that burst into civil war in Spain very quickly made that country the principal theater in which a world-wide tragedy was unfolding. The terrible bloodletting of 1914–1918, the Depression, the rise of communism and fascism had all loosed desperate fears in Europe. The nations, steeped in suspicion and hatred of each other, were shaken by internal troubles and awaited with dreadful foreboding a new world war.

France, in which a Fascist uprising was only narrowly avoided, had elected a mildly Socialist government in June, 1936. Torn by political opportunism, exhausted by her terrible losses during the First World War, she huddled behind her Maginot Line and stared apprehensively at her ancient enemy across the Rhine.

Britain, where memories of a general strike were still vivid, with a weak government and a huge if obsolescent navy, enjoyed a declining evening of empire and hoped that, if she shut her eyes tightly enough, Europe and its problems might simply vanish.

Italy, under the strutting Mussolini, had been the first country of Europe to embrace fascism. Rattling a sword, which was not yet known to be made of tin, Mussolini had outbluffed England and France to conquer Ethiopia. In place of any constructive social ideas he invited his people to embark on a comic-opera scheme for rebuilding the Roman Empire.

In Germany, the despair of defeat, the hysteria of militarism, and the hopelessness of the Depression had combined to bring Hitler to power. Solving the unemployment problem by concentrating on rebuilding a mighty war machine, the insane dictator, with the enthusiastic support of his sadistic followers, was busily converting Germany into a bellicose lunatic asylum.

Russia, which had suffered untold millions of casualties in the First World War, two revolutions, a long civil war, and vast famines, had not quite given up hope of a world-wide Communist revolution. But under the ruthless leadership of Josef Stalin, the nation was now concentrating on industrialization, preparation for an inevitable war, and the huge purges by which the paranoid dictator was to wipe out hundreds of thousands of suspected domestic enemies.

The League of Nations had proved itself powerless to halt aggression and was now looked upon as little more than a debating society. The only effective international organization of the period was the vast and complex Communist network known as the Comintern. Organized by men of great ability and fanatic devotion in nearly every country of the world, the Comintern had originally been intended as the spearhead of world revolution. But with the rise of fascism and its threat of open war against the

Soviet Union, Stalin ordered the Comintern to devote itself to cooperation with Western democratic parties and governments, for the Russians would need allies in any struggle with fascism. It was for this reason that Communist parties throughout the world supported coalition left-wing governments where they arose and refrained from undermining conservative governments where they existed. All differences were to be submerged in the common fight against fascism.

And if all Europe had a stake in the outcome of the Spanish Civil War, it should be remembered that no one intervened in Spain until the Spaniards themselves requested intervention.

On the night of July 19, with cities in flames throughout Spain, Prime Minister José Giral, not trusting his diplomatic corps, telegraphed directly to Léon Blum, Socialist Premier of France, ". . . surprised by a dangerous military uprising. Beg of you to help us immediately with arms and airplanes. Fraternally yours, Giral."

On the night of July 20, General Franco dispatched Luis Bolin and Luca de Tena in the *Dragon Rapide* (still piloted by Captain Bebb) to Rome to seek assistance from Mussolini. Other emissaries were sent to Germany.

At first Léon Blum and his War Minister, Edouard Daladier, decided to help the Republic. As members of a Socialist government they too feared the consequences of a Fascist uprising. As Frenchmen they were even more concerned at the possibility of a Fascist government in Madrid completing a ring of enemies with Germany and Italy around France. Giral had asked for twenty bombers, a few machine guns and cannon, four million bullets, and twenty thousand bombs. But before Blum could act upon this request, the British Government intervened. Stanley Baldwin, Britain's Prime Minister, and Anthony Eden, his Foreign Secretary, feared that French help to the Republic would ignite a general European war—something they were then determined to avoid at any price. At a hurried meeting in London, Eden asked Blum, "Are you going to send arms to the Spanish Republic?" When Blum said yes, Eden answered, "It is your affair, but I ask you one thing. Be prudent."

That remark by Eden, "It is your affair," must have chilled Blum's heart. For the cornerstone of French foreign policy was its alliance with Britain. Knowing they could not fight Germany and Italy alone, the French were not willing to take any action which might endanger their alliance with the British Empire and Commonwealth. When, for example, Hitler marched back into the Rhineland and France prepared to fight, the French Government had backed down when they found that Britain would not support them.

When Blum returned to Paris, troubled by Eden's warning, he found the country ablaze over the arms transfer. "No one can understand," said one politician, "why we are going to risk war on behalf of Spain when we did not do so over the Rhineland." Newspapers of the right flamed with angry headlines about the "gun-running government." In the Chamber of Deputies, former Premier Herriot cried, "Ah, I beg you, my son, I beg you not to get yourself involved down there!" Blum, whose heart went out to the Republic, found it impossible to ship it arms officially. But unofficially the French government henceforth shipped munitions to Mexico, they were then trans-shipped to Spain. Besides that, the Republic was permitted to purchase arms from private individuals freely in France. It was only after Italian and German intervention on Franco's side was definitely established that France officially shipped arms and a few technicians and pilots to Spain.

Meanwhile General Franco's envoys were meeting with Mussolini and his Foreign Secretary, Count Ciano. They informed Ciano that, with twelve transport planes to bring the Army of Africa to the mainland, the rebels could win the war in a few days. Mussolini agreed and immediately dispatched eleven Italian transport planes to Morocco. But this was only the beginning of an involvement that was to cost Italy thousands of lives, millions of pounds, and its military reputation. Why did Mussolini leap in? First of all, he was flattered by the request. Secondly, he hoped to see a Fascist Spain established on France's southern border. Finally, he simply wanted to demonstrate Italy's new military might to the world. "Italians," he proclaimed, "have to be kept up to the mark by kicks on the shins." It was, of course, the Italian people, who detested war and were much too civilized to make good Fascists, who had to pay for their dictator's lunacy. Italian "volunteers" in Spain at one time numbered 50,000, of whom over 6,000 were to die. The Italian Air Force, besides supplying 700 planes to the rebels, participated in 5,000 bombing raids on Republican targets. The Italian Navy sank over 72,000 tons of Republican shipping. And when the Spanish Civil War was almost ended, Mussolini remarked, "When the war in Spain is over, I shall have to find something else. The Italian character must be formed through fighting."

On July 26, General Franco's envoys to Germany met with Hitler and his henchmen. Hermann Goering was anxious to support the rebels so that his *Luftwaffe* could experience training under actual war conditions. Admiral Wilhelm Canaris hoped for a rebel victory so that German submarines would be able to use Spanish bases in the coming war against England and France. Hitler himself, although he hated General Franco's Catholicism almost as much as the Republic's socialism, was swayed only by practical considerations. Germany needed Spanish iron ore and a Fascist ally who could attack France from the south and close the Mediterranean to the British fleet. On Hitler's orders a special section was set up in the German War Office to help the rebels. Fifty-two Junker transport planes were sent immediately to Morocco. *Luftwaffe* pilots to the number of 14,000 were organized into the Condor Legion and rotated to Spain to fight—and to learn.

Such German specialist units as thirty anti-tank companies were sent along with other "volunteers" to the number of 10,000. While no one yet knows the exact amount of arms and munitions sent, it has been estimated at 50 million pounds worth.

During July and August, while France, Italy, and Germany were rushing aid to their respective sides in Spain, Russia and the international Comintern debated what to do. Stalin cared nothing for the fate of the tiny Spanish Communist party (or for any other foreign Communist party). He was concerned only about Russian interests. If, for example, Russia poured aid into the Republic, would not English and French conservatives grow fearful and would this not in turn destroy Russian efforts to seek an alliance against Hitler? On the other hand, a Fascist victory in Spain, by threatening France from the south, might paralyze her so that Hitler would feel free to attack Russia without fear of French attack from the rear. Stalin, cautiously and slowly, finally concluded that he would help the Republic just enough to make sure it did not lose—but not enough to assure it of victory. It was not until late October that Russian aid reached the Republic, and then only after most of the nation's gold had been transferred to the Soviet Union to assure payment. Nevertheless, there is no doubt that Russian aid did save the Republic time and again from defeat. Unable to purchase arms from the Western democracies, the Republican government was forced into greater and greater reliance upon the Communists. It has been estimated that during the Civil War Russia sent the Spanish Republic over 240 air-planes, 700 cannon, 730 tanks, and 29,000 tons of munitions, as well as nearly 1,000 "volunteer" specialists and advisors.

Britain, having prevented France from supporting the Republic directly, was itself torn by passionate debate on the Civil War. The Labor party, as well as trade unions, intellectuals, writers, and artists, demanded aid for the Republic. Newspapers, magazines, and public speakers deluged the country with propaganda

for one side or the other. British youths volunteered, mainly
for the Republican militia, and humanitarian societies gathered
large sums for relief of the Republicans. Conservatives, on the
other hand, eager to appease Hitler and Mussolini and deeply
suspicious of Russia, kept the country from sending any active
support.

The United States, already absorbed in the excitement of Franklin D. Roosevelt's second election campaign, remained staunchly
isolationist. Although the American Ambassador to Spain, Claude
Bowers, Roosevelt himself, and most of his official staff were
strongly sympathetic to the Republic, Congress and the American
people still believed that oceans would suffice to keep unpleasant
realities from their shores. Congress had passed the Neutrality
Act, which made it illegal for Americans to sell arms to belligerents anywhere. Bowing to Secretary of State Cordell Hull's advice,
Roosevelt was forced to clamp an embargo on arms for either side
in Spain. But, as in England, the passions aroused by the Spanish
Civil War stirred up furious storms in America. The press, magazines, books, and radio poured forth argument and propaganda
for both sides. Funds were raised for relief, and volunteers set out
to join the Republic. The *New York Times* sent correspondents
to both sides in Spain and found that each became desperately
committed to the side he covered.

But of all the foreign involvement in the Spanish Civil War,
nothing so caught the imagination of the world as the formation
of the International Brigades. These volunteer troops were raised
by Communist parties throughout the world and organized by
the Comintern. About eighty percent of the volunteers either were
Communists or became Communists—the rest were Socialists,
liberals, non-political adventurers. But all were idealists. For these
were the days before the Hitler-Stalin pact, the days before it was
generally known what Stalin had done to Russia. These were days
when it seemed to many people that only the Communists were

prepared to really fight fascism. The young men of the International Brigades overwhelmingly fought and bled in what they conceived as a crusade against fascism. One of Stalin's most treacherous crimes was his cold-blooded misuse of their heroism for ends of which they had not the faintest idea. The great English poet W. H. Auden, who himself enlisted in an ambulance unit, has described the eagerness with which they answered Spain's call for help:

> *Many have heard it on remote peninsulas,*
> *On sleepy plains, in the aberrant fishermen's islands*
> *   In the corrupt heart of the city,*
> *Have heard and migrated like gulls or the seeds of a flower.*
> *They clung like burrs to the long expresses that lurch*
> *Through unjust lands, through the night, through the alpine*
> *   tunnel;*
> *   They floated over the oceans;*
> *They walked the passes: they came to present their lives.*

The Communist party in each country had been assigned a quota of volunteers to be raised. These men, singly or in small groups, were usually sent first to Comintern headquarters in Paris. From there they were shipped by train to the International Brigade base at Albacete in Spain. Here they were issued uniforms, organized into companies and battalions according to nationality, rigorously trained, and dosed with propaganda. Eventually there were five International Brigades in Spain, and over 40,000 men served in them at one time or another. There were battalions of Frenchmen, Hungarians, Italian anti-Fascists, German anti-Nazis, Yugoslavs, Czechoslovakians, Poles, and even Albanians. There were a British, a Canadian, and two American Battalions—the Lincoln Battalion and the Washington Battalion.

These men, well-trained and well-armed, led by internationally renowned generals (many of whom later rose to positions of great power in the Communist world—Marshal Tito of Yugoslavia, Premier Dimitrov of Bulgaria, Ulbricht of East Germany, and Togliatti, head of the Italian Communist party), were to give a good account of themselves in the fighting to come. They suffered very high casualties, but on more than one occasion saved the Republic from defeat.

And if the Spanish Civil War attracted youthful idealists, it also attracted the world's leading writers, poets, and artists. Most, though not all, of these supported the Republic. Ernest Hemingway served in a Republican ambulance unit and later wrote *For Whom The Bell Tolls,* based on his long and passionate adherence to the Republic. André Malraux, the great French writer, trained pilots for the Republican Air Force and personally flew on bombing missions. A poll taken in England revealed that only five writers, among them Evelyn Waugh, supported Franco. T. S. Eliot and Ezra Pound remained neutral on principle, while Samuel Beckett answered the poll by simply scrawling "UPTHEREPUB-LIC" in capital letters. Overwhelmingly, from W. H. Auden to Rebecca West, from Aldous Huxley to Sean O'Casey, artists and intellectuals supported the Republic.

But while artists issued flaming pronouncements, while young men rushed to volunteer, while diplomats scurried through Europe's corridors, while dictators schemed and lied, the Spanish people plunged into battle—and in spite of many brave words, it soon appeared that the Republic would quickly lose.

IV

The First Campaigns

AT first it was hard to find a battle line in Spain. Rebels and Republicans faced each other in isolated places: on the outskirts of certain cities, sometimes across narrow roads, sometimes across wide valleys. On bleak hilltops outside Republican villages, armed workers—militiamen without uniforms and with fewer rifles than men—would huddle around their nightly campfires and stare at similar fires sparkling in the night around them, often without knowing whether these pinpoints of light indicated friends or enemies. In those early days, thousands who had found themselves on the wrong side of the "front" found it easy to pass through the lines and rejoin their friends.

The rebel forces were divided, both organizationally and geographically, into two overall commands. In the north, with fronts facing east towards Barcelona, north towards the Basque country, and south towards Madrid, General Emilio Mola commanded a mixed group of Regular Army units, Falangists, Monarchist bands, and local *Guardia Civil.* In the south, with mopping-up operations to be conducted throughout Andalusia and with fronts facing southeast to Málaga, west to the Portuguese border, and north to Madrid, General Franco had established himself in command at Seville. The rebel forces, being better trained and armed and enjoying unity of command, maintained strict discipline as they prepared for immediate offensives.

The Republicans at first were completely disorganized. There was a central command at Madrid, but the Catalans fighting in Aragon received independent orders from Barcelona, the Basques in the north operated completely separately, and many of the cities on the Mediterranean paid little heed to instructions from Madrid. Trade unions and political parties had armed their own men and rushed them to the "front." Once there they continued to think of themselves as Socialists, Anarchists, Liberals, or Communists first and Republicans second. In many cases they simply refused to cooperate.

In Aragon, for example, which was left to the responsibility of the semi-independent government of Catalonia, the "front" ran southwards from the foothills of the Pyrenees Mountains and was held at some points by members of a Socialist trade union, at others by a rival Socialist trade union, and at still others by Anarchists. The "battle line" here would consist of a group of men on a lightly fortified hill on the outskirts of some village in which reinforcements and possibly a few cannon supported them. Neither the troops nor the commanders had much contact with other Republican columns. The Socialist column established headquarters at Tardienta. When some of their men looted the town

77

Spain, August, 1936 (Shaded areas indicate Nationalist regions)

and attempted to send back the spoils in trucks to Barcelona, they were halted by soldiers from the rival trade union column, tried as thieves, and shot. Their bodies were returned to Tardienta in coffins. The most powerful Republican force in this area was the Anarchist column, commanded by Buenaventura Durruti, a former Anarchist gunman who had helped assassinate the Archbishop of Saragossa years before. On their march to the "front," the Anarchists had passed through the town of Lérida. Here, although the citizens were fervently Republican, they had decided to spare their beautiful cathedral. Durruti soon put that right—the cathedral was burned. But his violence worked against him. In several localities his men were forced to withdraw because of the growing hatred of the peasants.

Saragossa was the primary Republican objective on this front. It was held by Army regulars, Falangists, and Monarchists. And although the Republicans were close enough to see the lights of the city twinkling at night, they were never to capture it.

In the mountains north of Madrid, the Republican militia tried to behave more like soldiers than their comrades in Aragon. On this vital front even the Anarchists were known to obey orders occasionally. The militia held all but two of the high mountain passes leading south to Madrid. They had rifles and a few machine guns, little artillery, and were identifiable by the trade union insignia sewn onto their caps. Under the command of a Republican Regular Army officer, Major Perea, they were organized into battalions of about six hundred men each. These battalions often took the name of some old revolutionary battle (there was a "Commune de Paris" battalion), or of some Republican leader (there was a "La Pasionaria" battalion). They were opposed in the high mountains by rebel troops who, due to lack of ammunition, made no attempt to advance against them.

The most effective unit north of Madrid was undoubtedly the Fifth Regiment, organized by the Communist party. These troops tried hard to make themselves into soldiers. They learned how to march in step by hiring the Madrid Municipal Band to play for them. Eight thousand volunteers, recruited largely by *La Pasionaria,* fought in this regiment which had instituted a system of political commissars for each company. This device, borrowed from the Russian Red Army, was intended to ensure the loyalty of officers and to douse the troops with propaganda. No order was theoretically valid unless countersigned by a commissar.

It was from the ranks of the Fifth Regiment that some of the Republic's most famous military commanders emerged. There were Enrique Lister, a former quarryman, and Juan Modesto, an ex-woodcutter. Both of these able soldiers had fought in the Asturias uprising, escaped to Russia, and there trained at the Frunze Military Academy. Another leader emerged in the person of Valentín González, known always as *El Campesino* (the peasant). He was famed for his huge and powerful physique, his talkativeness, and his bushy beard. He claimed to have earned his nickname by blowing up four members of the *Guardia Civil* in a sentry box when a boy and then hiding among the peasants in the hills. He also claimed to have fought on both sides in Morocco. Although a brilliant guerrilla leader, he found himself beyond his depth when later he rose to command a division.

The rebel commanders launched two well-conceived campaigns at the beginning of August, 1936. In the north General Mola attacked to cut the Basques off from the French frontier, while in the south General Franco marched to isolate the Republic from Portugal and link up with Mola's forces in the north.

The transport of Franco's Army of Africa to the mainland had been accomplished by German and Italian transport planes and by merchant ships protected by Italian fighter planes. The Republican fleet units in the Straits of Gibraltar, incompetently run by their crews, abandoned control of the Straits and fled to the harbors of Cartagena and Barcelona, where they remained for the

rest of the war. Thousands of legionnaires and Moroccans were therefore able to reach the mainland from Morocco at a vital moment.

The Army of Africa, under the overall command of General Franco in Seville, was commanded in the field by General Juan de Yagüe—a brilliant and hard-hitting officer of the Foreign Legion. Beneath him were columns commanded by Colonels Carlos Asensio, Antonio Castejón, and Cantos Tella—all veteran fighters. Each column was composed of a mixed group of legionnaires and Moroccans with artillery support. Their advance north from Seville was the world's first *blitzkrieg*. Roaring up the road in trucks, the columns would halt when they reached a Republican-held village. While the troops waited, artillery would bombard the place for thirty minutes. Then the legionnaires and Moroccans would fight their way into the town, hunt out and shoot Republicans, climb back into their trucks, and race on to the next town. Yagüe's men advanced two hundred and fifty miles in this way in less than a week. It was not until they reached the city of Mérida that they met any determined Republican resistance. Here the Republican militia fought a sharp, short battle and then fled. With the capture of this city Yagüe had succeeded in the first of Franco's objectives: he had linked up with the rebels in the north. Now he turned to accomplish his second objective— cutting off the Portuguese frontier.

The city of Badajoz, ancient, heavily walled, and protected by the river Guadiana, was Republican Spain's last outpost near Portugal. It was under the command of Colonel Ildefonso Puigdendolas. He had just been reinforced by two thousand militiamen from Madrid. With the local Republican forces his command totaled five thousand—far more than Yagüe could bring against him. But just before Yagüe's men attacked, the *Guardia Civil* within the city rebelled and were only put down after heavy fighting. After an artillery bombardment that lasted all morning, Yagüe ordered his men against the walls of the city. A unit of the Foreign Legion, singing their hymn to death, fought their way through the main gates only to be repulsed by Republican machine guns. But they attacked again, stabbing their way in with knives and forcing an entry. Of this assault unit only sixteen men survived—but they were within the city. At the same time another unit of legionnaires stormed a different section of the walls. After sharp fighting the two units met in front of the cathedral. Thereafter the city was lost. Sharp street fighting merged into plain murder as legionnaires and Moroccans fought wildly and under no command. All armed militiamen were shot on sight. Many who had been disarmed were thrown into the city's bull ring and shot later. Badajoz became a city of corpses—and the Republic lost its last contact with the Portuguese frontier.

On August 20, Yagüe resumed his march. But this time he headed east towards Madrid. Over the mountains and down through the parched valley of the river Tagus came the Army of Africa. Before it the Republic's hastily organized Army, under General Manuel Riquelme, continued to retreat. Although a squadron of French planes commanded by André Malraux succeeded in destroying a rebel column in the city of Medellín, the Republican militiamen on the ground were no match for the legionnaires and Moroccans. Time and again they were outmaneuvered and forced to retreat from easily defensible positions. Some militiamen deserted. Most refused to dig trenches, for they considered that undignified and cowardly. Matters were not helped by the fact that the Anarchists refused to obey General Riquelme's orders and wasted their strength making attacks in the wrong direction. On September 2, the Army of Africa reached the town of Talavera de la Reina. There they found ten thousand militiamen supported by artillery and holding good defensive positions before the town. At dawn the legionnaires seized the airfield and the railroad station; at midday they assaulted the city itself and, after very little street fighting, forced the Republicans to flee. The last town of importance between Franco's forces and Madrid had fallen.

The efficiency and experience of the Army of Africa explained much of the rebel success. Republican militiamen who showed great bravery in street battles found themselves out-maneuvered in open country by the legionnaires. And the inexperienced militia were terrified by aerial bombardment. One or two bombers, even when they completely missed their target, could often cause a general panic and rout among the militia forces. The rebel commanders were also superior to their Republican opposites. They were constantly able to force the militia to choose between being surrounded and retreating. The Republic lacked rifles for training and lacked any decent central control staff. Those Regular Army officers who had remained loyal to the Republic searched about desperately for some precedent in the problem of leading inexperienced mass armies. Their principal guide was the Russian Revolution—but that was inapplicable to conditions in Spain.

While General Franco's Army thus advanced rapidly from the south, General Mola's forces faced bitter fighting in the north. Mola sought to cut off the Basque country from possible French help by capturing the cities of Irún and San Sebastián at the western end of the Pyrenees on the French border. An important objective at Irún was the International Bridge crossing the river into France at Hendaye.

On August 17, rebel warships (including the *Almirante Cevera* and the *España* captured at El Ferrol, where their Republican crews had all been shot) began a naval bombardment of San Sebastián. While the civil population hid in cellars, the Basque commander threatened to execute his rebel hostages unless the ships withdrew. When they did not he began executing rebels. Italian bombers also joined in the bombardment daily. But the population did not panic and Mola transferred his attack to Irún.

On August 26, the land assault on Irún was ordered. In command of the rebel troops there was Colonel Alfonso Beorlegui, who had two thousand men, including five hundred legionnaires, under him. He also enjoyed all the artillery support that Mola could scrape together as well as a few light tanks. Opposing him in Irún were three thousand Basques who had few rifles, no tanks, and no artillery. They did, however, have the support of a few French specialist volunteer units. The battle for Irún was fought so close to the French border that Colonel Beorlegui had to warn his men against firing to the east. Day after day would open with a rebel artillery barrage, followed by an assault. But later the Republicans would counterattack and win back their lost positions. Then the rebel artillery bombardment would start all over again. The Puntza bridge, for instance, was captured and recaptured four times before the rebels finally held it.

At the customs house on the outskirts of Irún, the Republicans, after those who could had jumped into the river to swim to France, fought to the last man. By September, most of the civilian population of Irún had fled into France. Pushing their belongings in baby carriages, carrying their household goods on their backs, demoralized and bitter, they were the first trickle of what was to become a mighty torrent of refugees trudging all the roads of Europe in the next decade. On September 3, Beorlegui, with fifteen hundred men, made a final assault on Irún. While huge crowds of spectators watched from the French side of the border, the rebels were at first repulsed. By two in the morning, however, Republican resistance had crumbled and the militia began to retreat over the International Bridge into France. The Anarchists stayed last. They set fire to parts of the city and executed some of the political prisoners in Fort Guadalupe. Then they escaped over the bridge. All militiamen who wished it (five hundred did) were transported by the French back to Barcelona, where they could continue the struggle. Colonel Beorlegui's men conquered a ruined and abandoned city. The Colonel himself was killed by fire from a French Communist volunteer machine gun unit at the very approach to the International Bridge.

San Sebastián, holding out until September 13, was surrendered finally by the Basques who feared the destruction of that beautiful city (certain Anarchists who wished to set fire to the city when the rebels entered were shot by the Basque Republicans)—and General Mola's objective was thus secured. From then on the Basques, cut off from France, would fight in complete isolation, with only the sea to their backs.

While Generals Mola and Franco were thus carrying through their plans to cut off the Republic and converge on Madrid, the rebel General José Varela, operating under Franco, led his Moroccan troops on a swift consolidation of the rebel positions in Andalusia. The countryside around the cities of Cordova, Seville, Granada, Cadiz, and Algeciras was quickly subdued. But before these troops could launch an attack upon the Republican seaport stronghold of Málaga, they were themselves attacked by Republican forces under General José Miaja, a Regular Army officer who had briefly been commander of all Republican forces. Leading ten thousand Andalusian militiamen, Miaja reached the gates of Cordova. But General Varela arrived with his Moroccan troops before the city fell, launched a counterattack, and drove the Republicans in disorder from the field.

Another Republican campaign met with greater success. On the ninth of August a Catalan and Valencian expeditionary force set out from Barcelona, convoyed by destroyers and submarines, to conquer the Balearic Islands, where the rebel uprising had been successful on July 19. The expedition was led by Captain Alberto Bayo of the Republican Air Force, who had been trained at West Point. They landed first on the island of Ibiza and quickly conquered it with the help of the local peasants who rose against the rebel governor. Then, still convoyed by the warships, Bayo's ten

General Miaja

thousand militiamen landed on the main island, Majorca. There
the landings were also successful—too successful, as the Republicans seemed confused by their easy victory and delayed too long
in moving inland from their beachhead. Soon they found themselves under bombardment by Italian planes and under attack by
units of the Foreign Legion. On September 3, under heavy rebel
pressure, the militiamen rushed back to their boats and abandoned
the island, leaving most of their equipment behind. Thereafter
Majorca became the most important base and staging area for
Italian planes and submarines fighting against the Republic in the
Mediterranean. Captain Bayo himself was later reported dead on
the Madrid front, but, many years later, he reappeared—as Chief
of Staff to Fidel Castro!

Meanwhile the rebels holding out in Gijón, Oviedo, and Toledo against large Republican besieging forces continued their resistance. In Gijón the rebels numbered only one hundred and eighty men and were besieged in the Simancas Barracks of that city. But their attackers had no arms or equipment except for dynamite—for these were the Asturian miners. The rebel commander in the barracks was Colonel Pinilla. The only help he received was from rebel warships that bombarded the rest of this Republican-held city. The rebels in Simancas Barracks were driven half mad by thirst; Colonel Pinilla's two sons, captured by the Republicans, were brought forward to tell their father that if he refused to surrender they would be executed. The Colonel refused—and they were shot. Finally, the miners, armed only with their dynamite, stormed the barracks. Pinilla ordered his men not to surrender, and when at the last moment he was being overwhelmed, he

radioed to the rebel warships, "Defense is impossible. The barracks are burning and the enemy is starting to enter. Fire on us!" The warships obeyed this command, and the defenders of the Simancas Barracks perished in flames.

At Toledo the resistance of the rebels in the ancient fortress of the Alcázar attracted the attention of the world. The old stronghold seemed impregnable. Constant rifle fire was exchanged between the defenders and the Republican assault troops all through August—with the rebels proving to be excellent marksmen. Insults were exchanged during the night and during the hot afternoon *siesta* hours by means of megaphones. Republican bombs dropped on the fortress seemed to have little effect. Although the defenders had plenty of ammunition, they had little food. They were forced to kill and eat the mules and then the horses (all except one, which was cared for as if he were a thoroughbred throughout the siege). Saltpeter was scraped from the walls for salt. Worst of all, the besieged rebels had no way of knowing what was happening in the rest of Spain until a rebel plane finally dropped leaflets over them advising them of Yagüe's advance up the valley of the Tagus. But the defenders behaved with traditional Spanish courage and bravado. *Fiestas* were even held in the basement of the fortress with *flamenco* singing and dancing. By September 13, the bread ration in the Alcázar had dropped to about seven ounces per day per person—but to Republican demands for surrender Colonel Ituarte Moscardó turned a deaf ear. He did, however, request that a priest be sent in, and the Republicans complied under a flag of truce on September 11. By this time defenders and besiegers felt they were old acquaintances. The *Guardia Civil* within received cigarettes from the Republicans and were permitted to send out messages to their families.

The Republicans, maddened by Moscardó's continued resistance, now planned to blast their way into the Alcázar by planting huge mines under each of its two towers. Foreign correspondents were invited to witness the blowing up of these towers as if it were a theatrical performance. But when, on September 18, the Republicans ignited the mines, only one exploded. The southeast tower fell—and it had little effect on the spirit of the defenders, who continued to resist from the rubble. Four rebel officers armed with pistols drove the militiamen from the ruins of this tower. Then, on September 20, the walls of the Alcázar were sprayed with petrol and other inflammable liquids. A grenade was duly tossed to ignite it, but the resulting fire again had little effect on the defenders, who were burrowed deep within the bedrock foundation of the fort.

On September 21, General Franco decided to drive on Toledo to lift the siege of the Alcázar. He was warned that by diverting his forces from the drive on Madrid he might lose his opportunity to capture the Republican capital. But Franco replied that the spiritual effects of rescuing the garrison of the Alcázar were more important than the conquest of Madrid. He ordered General José Varela to lead his columns to Toledo.

On September 25, the mine under the Alcázar's northeast tower was exploded. By this time the defenders could see Varela's men assembling to assault the city. On that same day the Republican militia broke and fled before Varela's Moroccans and legionnaires. As the rebels entered the city they discovered the mutilated bodies of two rebel airmen. For this reason they killed all Republican troops found in Toledo. Forty Anarchists trapped in a seminary set the place on fire and died in the flames rather than surrender.

When Varela himself entered Toledo on September 28, he found Colonel Moscardó and his half-starved men standing at attention before the ruins of the Alcázar. Moscardó saluted and reported with the words, "sin novedades" (nothing new).

In the meantime, the proximity of rebel forces to Madrid was brought home to the inhabitants of the Republican capital through

Spain, October, 1936 (Shaded areas indicate Nationalist regions)

air raids. These were mostly carried out by German planes. Soon air raid wardens were appointed for each block in the city, street lights were blacked out, sirens shrieked through the night, and many civilians died. These air raids were, of course, merely the forerunners of the terrible raids that were to reduce so much of Europe to rubble during the Second World War. British, French, German, and Italian observers studied the effects of the raids impartially to see what they could learn for use at home. As in so many other things, the people of Spain paid in blood for lessons that the rest of Europe had yet to comprehend. Apart from the damage and deaths caused by these raids, they also served as a warning that the nearby rebel forces would not long delay their attack upon the capital. Madrid's hour of truth was at hand.

V

The Siege of Madrid

EARLY in October, 1936, General Emilio Mola, in supreme command of rebel forces in the north, announced to reporters that he expected to enjoy his morning coffee at a café on Madrid's Gran Vía by October 12. Mola's optimism was understandable. With a record of continued success behind them, the rebel armies now planned an overwhelming assault on the Republic's capital. Under the overall command of General Franco, three armies would converge on Madrid. From the north, under field command of General Juan de Yagüe, columns of Monarchists, Falangists, and legionnaires; from the south, under General José Varela, regiments of Moroccans; from the west, under Colonels Carlos

General Mola

Asensio and Heli Rolando de Tella, columns of the Army of Africa. When he was asked by foreign correspondents which of his four columns would take Madrid, General Mola smiled and replied that Madrid would be taken by a "fifth column" of rebel sympathizers within the city—thereby coining a term that was to haunt the world for many years.

The city the rebels prepared to attack now underwent a political upheaval. Under pressure of continual defeats and failure to secure aid from the Western democracies, the government of José Giral came to an end. President Azaña, on September 4, heeding the demands of the masses and pressure from the left-wing trade unions, called upon the Socialist leader Largo Caballero to form a government. Caballero agreed, provided the Communists would join. This the Communists at first refused to do. They felt they might be compromised by associating with a Socialist government.

THE CIVIL WAR IN SPAIN

But on orders from Moscow they finally agreed to join—the first time a Communist party anywhere in the world had joined a democratic government. And their support was essential, for by this time their tight discipline, the fighting qualities of their Fifth Regiment, and their anti-Fascist determination had become indispensable to any Republican government. Socialists, too—of all varieties—sank their differences to join Caballero's "Government of Victory." In the general enthusiasm with which this new government was greeted, the fact that Tomás Hernández, the Minister of Education, had once been convicted of the attempted murder of Indalecio Prieto, the Minister of Air and Marine, was happily forgotten. Only the Anarchists, sticking strictly to their ideals, refused to join the government—although they agreed to support it. In Catalonia, when the Anarchists did join the Catalan government, they immediately began to lose their influence. The Anarchist leader Buenaventura Durruti, still commanding a column on the Aragon front, when interviewed by a Canadian foreign correspondent, expressed himself in words that have often been quoted since. The Canadian had warned him that if the Anarchists were victorious they would find themselves sitting on a pile of ruins. "We have always lived in slums and holes in the wall," Durruti replied. "We shall know how to accommodate ourselves for a time. It is we who built the palaces and cities here in Spain and in America and everywhere. We, the workers, can build cities to take their place. And better ones—we are not in the least afraid of ruins. We are going to inherit the earth. The *bourgeoisie* may blast and ruin their world before they leave the stage of history. But we carry a new world in our hearts."

With rebel armies closing in on their capital, with French aid too little and unreliable, the Republic felt itself abandoned. Fernando de los Ríos, the new Spanish ambassador in Washington, appealed to Secretary of State Cordell Hull to permit the Republic to buy arms in the United States. Strictly speaking, as a sovereign government, the Republic should have been entitled to buy arms anywhere in the world—while the rebels should not. But Cordell Hull, who had never demonstrated much faith in Spanish democracy, replied that America would hold to a policy of "moral aloofness." De los Ríos' accurate predictions that a Fascist victory in Spain would lead to the undermining of democracy throughout Europe went unheeded by Hull.

In Madrid, in preparation for the coming battle, Caballero's government tried to impose some sort of order on the chaotic Republican military organization. The various trade union and political militias were unified under the command of a central general staff. Political commissars were now appointed for all units in emulation of the Communist Fifth Regiment. But most important of all, on October 15, the first Russian shipments of arms reached the Republican ports of Alicante and Cartagena. Hundreds of cannon, tanks, planes, millions of rounds of ammunition, hundreds of specialists and technicians began to pour into the Republic. But would they reach the front in time to save Madrid?

On October 17, Largo Caballero telephoned to the vital road junction of Illescas, only about twenty miles from Madrid. He knew that a battle had occurred there and was anxious to know the results. To his horror, the phone was answered by rebel General Varela himself. A counterattack by the weary Republican militia made some advances and was then repelled. On October 20, still another Republican attack was led by General Torrado. With fifteen thousand men who had been transported to the front in Madrid's double-decker buses, he recaptured Illescas. But rebel forces from Toledo once again outflanked the militia, and they were forced to retreat.

The sound of battle could now be heard very clearly in Madrid. The city was sunk in gloomy despair. President Azaña, assuming that the capital was as good as lost, fled to Barcelona without

bothering to inform the government. When the Cabinet heard that Spain's President was now a resident of the monastery at Montserrat, outside Barcelona, it issued an announcement that he had left for an "extended tour of the fronts"—thus providing the people of Madrid with something to laugh about. But Largo Caballero's government had more immediate worries. General Emilio Mola's hint regarding a fifth column inside the city had been, they knew, no idle boast. A committee was set up to deal with possible fifth columnists. Once again murders swept the city. On October 24, General Luis Castello, who had gone insane, was relieved of command in Madrid and his post given to General Miaja, the old war horse of Cordova. In an attempt to rouse the population, Largo Caballero broadcast over Radio Madrid, "Our power of taking the offensive is growing. We have at our disposal a formidable mechanized armament. We have tanks and powerful airplanes. Listen, comrades! At dawn, our artillery and armored trains will open fire. Immediately, our aircraft will attack. Tanks will advance on the enemy at his most vulnerable point." Madrileños had heard these boasts before—but this time they were surprised to find them at least partly true.

On October 29, at dawn, a Russian tank force, driven by Russian technicians and led by the Russian tank specialist General Pavlov, smashed into the rebel cavalry units at Esquivas, in the outskirts of Madrid. In the fighting that followed, the rebel horsemen were scattered. But because the Fifth Regiment could not advance quickly enough to keep up with the tanks, this victory was empty. Esquivas was evacuated, and the main rebel advance continued to tighten a noose around Madrid.

On November 5, rebel forces entered the Madrid suburbs of Alcorcón and Leganés, where the bus and streetcar lines of the city ended. General Franco announced that the conquest of the city was at hand and advised its population to remain within their houses. Lists of prominent persons to be arrested had already been prepared, a municipal government for the city was waiting to take over in Avila, and long lines of trucks full of food for the population waited to enter behind the conquering armies. The world waited to hear of Franco's victorious entry.

Meantime, Largo Caballero's government (which at this fatal hour the Anarchists had finally joined) abandoned Madrid. Its leaders announced that it was impossible to carry on the government in a war zone and fled to the coastal city of Valencia. On the road they were turned back by Anarchist militiamen, but finally managed to make their escape. They left old General Miaja behind in command of the city.

The flight of Largo Caballero provided the Communists with a great opportunity. All along they had been the only ones who insisted that Madrid could be held. It was the voice of *La Pasionaria* that Madrileños heard night after night chanting, "No pasarán! No pasarán!" from their radios; it was the Communist-dominated councils of workers who now erected street barricades, dug trenches, and converted buildings into fortresses. While Russian-made planes dropped leaflets on the city urging continued resistance, the Communists set an example by putting themselves and their famous Fifth Regiment entirely at General Miaja's disposal.

As the people of the city, fired with new determination, prepared to resist, the rebels began nightly and daily air raids over the city. German and Italian bombers turned Madrid into an inferno. Thousands were killed and many more thousands made homeless. The Russian fighter planes could not prevent these raids, though Russian, German, and Italian observers learned much by studying their effects. One thing they might have learned was that terror bombing, far from cowing the civilian population, only infuriated it. Daily, by the thousands, Madrid's workers, men, women, and children, marched down the streets with shovels and axes to work on the trenches and defenses. A women's infantry company was formed and later fought heroically. While Madrid burned, Spanish Republican broadcasters warned the world that the same fate lay in store for London, Berlin, Tokyo, Leningrad; but it seemed that the world was deaf to Spain's agony.

The rebel Generals Varela and Yagüe were about to undertake a type of battle new to the pages of history. Their well-trained, well-equipped army of twenty thousand legionnaires and Moroccans was about to attack an ill-armed but huge urban mass population. Their plan was relatively simple. On the outskirts of Madrid rises University City. This is a complex of buildings built early in the century to house the University of Madrid. University City is perched atop a steep hill which looks down upon the narrow valley of the Manzanares River on the city's outskirts. The rebels planned to throw two columns across the river, have them scale the heights, seize University City, and enter Madrid proper. Meanwhile a diversionary attack by General Tella on the suburb

"No pasarán!" Nationalist troops attack at Illescas, outside Madrid.

of Carabanchel was to be made to draw Republican forces from the Casa del Campo, as the huge fields below University City were called.

The battle opened on November 7 with a large artillery bombardment. But when the rebel troops advanced to the Casa del Campo, the Republican militia opposing them fought like tigers. Inflamed by pamphlets and speeches, aware that the fall of Madrid would mean the doom of the Republic, the militia fought with terrible tenacity throughout the day. While Republican commanders, after reporting that half their men were dead, begged for reinforcements (which did not exist), thousands of workers rushed to the front. Many went without rifles, determined to pick up the guns of their dead comrades. When evening fell the rebels had made almost no gains. All night long Radio Madrid appealed for total mobilization—and all night long the long lines of wounded militiamen streamed in from the Casa del Campo. Ammunition was running dangerously low. At one point, indomitable old General Miaja actually issued blank cartridges to the men, feeling that soldiers who could still hear their rifles fire would continue to resist. As dawn of November 8 came, in spite of their heroic resistance of the preceding day, the Republican cause seemed hopeless. General Varela's artillery opened a new bombardment of University City. The militiamen steeled themselves for the coming assault.

But as Varela's guns battered Madrid, a new and startling spectacle presented itself to the beleaguered citizens. For there, marching down the Gran Vía in perfect precision, came pouring into the city units of the International Brigades. Swinging along with modern weapons, steel helmets, uniforms, and all the newly learned pride of real soldiers came German infantry, British machine-gunners, French and Belgian volunteers, Polish and Italian troops—all followed by two squadrons of French cavalry. Battalions with stirring names such as the "Commune de Paris," the

General "Kléber"

"Garibaldi," the "Edgar André," and the "Dabrowsky" showed the Madrileños that they were not fighting alone. The people went wild with joy. Shouts of "Salud!" and "No pasarán!" were answered by the Internationals with cries of "Rot front!" "Libertad!" and "Les Soviets partout!"

By evening the International Brigade was in position in and around University City. Some of its members were spread out among the Republican militia to give them heart and to teach them how to shoot. Now, for the first time, the Army of Africa ran into machine-gunning that was deadly accurate. Brigade Commander General Kléber was given command of all Republican forces in the Casa del Campo. Kléber, whose real name was Lazar Stern, had served as a captain in the Austrian Army during the First World War. Taken prisoner by the Russians, he had been liberated by the Bolsheviks during the Russian Revolution.

He turned Communist, attended various Russian military schools, and became one of the Comintern's chief agents. His efficiency and determination breathed new life into the Republican defense of Madrid.

Having been stopped in the Casa del Campo, General Varela now made a determined attack in the Carabanchel suburb. But his Moroccans became confused at street fighting in a large city, and they made very little progress. While they were attacking, General Kléber had gathered his Internationals together, and on the evening of November 9 they assaulted the rebel lines, crying, "For the revolution and liberty—forward!" The fighting lasted all night and into the following morning. By noon the rebels had been driven from the field—but a third of the International Brigade had been killed. The fighting in Carabanchel continued without letup for the next few days, and into it was sent the Second International Brigade, composed mainly of Germans, French, and Italians.

At this time a force of three thousand Anarchists also arrived to help defend Madrid. It was under the command of Durruti, who had rushed with his men from the Aragon front to fight for the nation's capital. Durruti demanded an independent front for his men so they would be able to show what they could do. General Miaja foolishly consented and allowed him to take over the Casa del Campo from the weary Internationals. Durruti was ordered to attack on November 15. All available Republican artillery and aircraft supported him. But when the hour came, the Anarchists, terrified by the Moroccan machine-gunning, refused to advance. Seizing his chance, General Varela immediately ordered a full-scale attack by rebel forces in the Casa del Campo. Three times the rebel troops fought their way across the river Manzanares, and three times they were thrown back. Finally, however, the Anarchists broke and fled. When the Moroccans reached the base of the hill below University City, they found no one to oppose them. They quickly scaled the hill and seized the School of Architecture and nearby buildings. The International Brigade was quickly rushed into the Hall of Philosophy and Letters—but meanwhile more and more of the Army of Africa was crossing the Manzanares.

A bloody and confused battle now exploded in University City. Hours of heavy artillery bombardment, during which neither side would break, were followed by ferocious hand-to-hand battles for the possession of a single room or some floor of a building. Commands in many different languages rang out among the Internationals to mix with the babble of Arabic. In the hospital building the German Internationals of the Thaelmann Battalion sent elevators loaded with grenades up to explode in the faces of the Moroccans on the floor above. A detachment of Poles died fighting to the last man against the legionnaires in the Casa de Velásquez building.

A detachment of Moroccans once again drove back Durruti's Anarchists to break through into the center of Madrid. But this small group was wiped out to the last man, as old General Miaja jumped into the battle line to stiffen the militia's courage, shouting, "Cowards! Die in your trenches! Die with your General Miaja!"

The fighting in University City raged on until November 23. By that time General Varela's men held three-quarters of the area, but could make no further advances. Both sides set about building fortifications, and the battle quieted down as both sides realized they could not afford the cost of winning a victory.

Baffled in their attempt to take Madrid by frontal assault, the rebel commanders now determined to cut it off from the rest of Spain by encirclement. The first move in this effort was an attempt to cut the main Corunna road leading northwest from the city. Assembling seventeen thousand men, Varela concentrated his attack on the little road junction of Boadilla del Monte. A heavy artillery bombardment prepared the way, and by nightfall the

town had fallen. The next day the International Brigades, supported by Russian-made tanks, drove the rebels from the town. But after the Polish and German battalions had entered the village, the rebels outflanked and then surrounded them. The fighting was savage, and only after suffering heavy casualties did the

Internationals retreat. But when the rebel commanders assessed the cost of the small gains they had made, they decided to call off further attacks. A definite stalemate had been reached in and around Madrid.

It has been said that the International Brigades saved Madrid. Perhaps, in the long run, they did. But it should never be forgotten that Varela's forces were stopped by the Republican militia in the Casa del Campo before the Internationals arrived. It was the people of Madrid who won the victory. Their determination, pride, and consciousness of the importance of their fight were expressed by a Republican deputy over Madrid Radio: "Here in Madrid is the universal frontier that separates liberty and slavery. . . . This is Madrid. It is fighting for Spain, for Humanity, for Justice, and with the mantle of its blood, it shelters all human beings! Madrid! Madrid!"

But perhaps the best commentary on the battle was provided by the sharp Madrileño sense of humor. For in response to General Mola's boast before the battle, a table at one of Madrid's cafes had been kept reserved for him with a large sign wondering when he was coming for his coffee. The General was never able to accept that invitation.

VI

Two Spains

WITHIN a few weeks of the rebellion, two very different yet similar Spains emerged behind the fighting lines. At first, under the pressure of constant battle, revolution, and the uncontrollable passions of individuals on both sides of the line, these two Spains showed themselves in their most extreme and violent colors. Outside observers, often heavily influenced by, or committed to, the political ideology of one side or the other, generally oversimplified what they saw. Sometimes they were guilty of outright lying; more often they saw what they expected or wanted to see. Holding firm to obsolete conceptions of how people who called themselves Anarchists, Communists, Socialists, Fascists, and Monarchists were *supposed* to act, many observers (though certainly not all) gave the world a picture of Spain that had little to do with actuality. And, as always when war intensifies loyalties and hatreds, many forgot that personal rather than political motives (especially in violently individualistic Spain) lay behind many events. Thus, General Franco was usually pictured as the perfect prototype of the Fascist; the salient fact that he was a devout Catholic was overlooked. The Spanish Communist party was always thought to have some clever reason for its errors when actually these were very often due to simple incompetence and poor leadership. As so often in the past, foreigners (who gave the world its picture of the Spanish Civil War) forgot that Spain's social and economic development, and hence its political evolution, were the result of an isolated and unique history. Slogans and words that might convey a certain meaning to the outside world often had very different meanings in a peninsula that historically had been as much influenced by Africa as by Europe.

Late in July, 1936, the rebels began to refer to themselves as Nationalists. In so doing they chose a name that described their movement with fair accuracy and postponed a definite decision as to what the organization of Spain would be if they won. Monarchists, supporting either of the pretenders to the throne, Falangists, the Church hierarchy, and, of course, the military, could unite under the broad banner and vague emotional appeal of Nationalism, each party convinced that with victory would come its opportunity to establish its own particular form of government. But in their schemings the parties reckoned without the ability and dedicated political insight of General Franco.

Of the four rebel generals who led the Nationalist uprising, Sanjurjo was killed in an airplane crash, Goded was executed by the Republicans in Barcelona, and Mola appeared quite willing to stand aside. Thus, General Franco was declared Head of State on October 1, 1936, in the ancient university town of Salamanca.

The speech he made on this occasion was an indication of his ideas for the future of Spain. The popular vote would be eliminated; labor would be protected against capital; the Church would regain a favored position; the economic independence of the peasants would be encouraged; and taxes would be more equitably distributed. But it was to be years before the "young general" could begin to effect this program, and much of it fell by the wayside. Meanwhile there were a civil administration to set up and a war to fight, and the terrible hatreds of the early days had to work themselves out.

Since almost all the civil servants and governors in Nationalist-held territory had been Republicans, civil administration was organized by the Army in cooperation with the *Falange*. High-ranking Republican political figures, trade unionists, civil governors, and Republican Army officers continued to be tried before military court-martials and generally executed for rebellion. For to the Nationalists, who considered themselves the true heirs of Spain's ancient ideals and customs, the Republicans were traitors. Under Nationalist military rule, strikes were declared illegal, all political parties with the exception of the *Falange* were banned, and all newspapers critical of the Nationalist cause were closed down. In many areas attendance at mass was all but compulsory. Public exhibition of religious fervor was supposed to mark the true Nationalist.

Spanish nationalism—like the nationalism of every other country—based itself on semi-mystical appeals to a glorious past. On August 15, 1936, in Seville, the Nationalists adopted the Monarchist crimson and gold flag as Spain's banner. Speaking from a balcony to a large crowd of supporters, General Franco kissed the flag and cried, "Here it is! It is yours! They wanted to rob us of it! This is our flag, one to which we have all sworn, for which our fathers have died a hundred times covered with glory!" On this occasion, too, the Nationalist poet José María Pemán expressed the emotional appeal of nationalism when he exclaimed, "Twenty centuries of Christian civilization are at our backs; we fight for love and honor, for the paintings of Velásquez, for the comedies of Lope de Vega, for Don Quixote and El Escorial!" And if these words made no reference to the continuing social and economic problems of Spain, if they might just as well have been shouted by any Republican orator, they nevertheless achieved their purpose of arousing popular enthusiasm.

The Nationalists succeeded from the beginning (except among the Basques) in winning the support of the Catholic Church both in Spain and abroad. Although there were some priests who sided with the Republic and some who, in Nationalist Spain, objected to political executions carried out in the name of Christ, the hierarchy overwhelmingly prayed for a Nationalist victory. Pope Pius XI spoke of the Republicans as having a "truly satanic hatred of God." Later, disgusted by some aspects of the Spanish hierarchy's fanaticism, the Pope was to show himself cool to the Nationalist cause. But throughout the war the Vatican could generally be counted upon to support Nationalist Spain. In those areas under Nationalist control divorces and civil marriages concluded under the Republic were annulled.

The Monarchists, among whose medieval-minded followers (consisting for the most part of fanatical Navarrese peasants) the worst atrocities were committed, spent much of their energy quarreling among themselves. The continued exile of Alfonso XIII and his son Don Juan greatly weakened their cause.

The *Falange*, now the only political organization permitted in Nationalist Spain, had been small but idealistic at the beginning of the Civil War. In many places its members were able to set up some sort of civilian justice to replace the harsh military court-martials. But with the Nationalist advance its ranks suddenly expanded to hundreds of thousands. Many of these new members were simply opportunists. Slowly but inevitably the *Falange* lost

its ideological importance and became an administrative police
organization whose members prowled the streets shouting, "Ar-
riba España!" (Up Spain!) without any clear idea of what a
Falangist was supposed to be. But if the party lost much of its
original purpose, it was now to provide a martyr and inspiration
to itself and to the entire Nationalist cause.

José Antonio Primo de Rivera, founder and leader of the
Falange, had been imprisoned in Alicante just before the uprising.
The Republican authorities there now put him on trial for treason.
The proceedings were rushed through for fear that if the Nationalists won a quick victory, José Antonio might go unpunished. The
trial itself, though the charges could probably have been proved
objectively, was a travesty of justice. José Antonio acted as his
own defense counsel. At one point he asked a militiaman who was
in the stand for the prosecution, "Do you hate the defendant?"
"With all my heart," the witness replied.

Needless to say, José Antonio, after a dignified and very elo-
quent defense, was condemned to death. The tribunal sentenced
his brother Miguel and his brother's wife to the same penalty. But
José Antonio appealed for their lives. "Life," he declared, "is not
a firework one lets off at the end of a garden party." As a result,
they were reprieved. José Antonio himself, dignified to the last,
was shot on November 19. His last request was that the prison

Falange Symbol

patio in which he was to be shot should be cleansed afterwards "so that my brother Miguel will not have to walk in my blood." Although he may have welcomed a conspiracy to overthrow the Republic, it remained unproven that he was an active plotter. The followers of José Antonio, with no justification apart from a desire for vengeance, murdered the son of the Republican Prime Minister Largo Caballero in reprisal, although he was only a prisoner of war.

With much of the old leadership eliminated, General Franco was able to take increasing control. Nationalist headquarters were established in Salamanca and Burgos, and Franco undertook a policy of playing Church, Army, and *Falange* off against each other in much the same manner as he had so successfully dealt with the Moorish chieftains in Morocco years before. Combined with his great caution and an uncanny political instinct, this policy was to be successful beyond all expectation. But if the world mistook the General for a simple Fascist, or perhaps only another strong man in the Spanish tradition, the years were to reveal some surprises. In the chaos of political hatreds which preceded the Second World War, a cynical world could not believe that Franco was just what he proclaimed himself to be: a deeply devout, sternly authoritarian, tradition-minded, intensely proud Spanish patriot. His own followers, as well as his allies and enemies, had much to learn about Franco.

While the Nationalists were thus organizing their section of the country, Republican Spain was still coping with the aftereffects of the revolution that had swept it after the arming of the workers in July, 1936. The Communist party became more and more important in the affairs of the nation. This was due not only to the fact that Russian aid was undoubtedly preserving the Republic from defeat and that Russian advisors and specialists were installing themselves in key positions throughout the country but to the relentlessly efficient and ruthless Communist attitude of winning the war first and discussing reform afterwards. The logic of this position was hammered home to Republicans with every battle. Even General Miaja, a Regular Army officer, admitted, "I like the Communists because they are more resolute. The Socialists talk first, then act. If the Communists talk, they do so *after* acting. Militarily speaking, it is an advantage."

But not everyone yet in the Republic was willing to speak only militarily, even under the pressures of civil war. The Anarchists still could not make up their minds to discipline themselves in support of the government in many areas. As a result of their attitude and their competition for the minds of Spanish peasants and workers, the Anarchists became the prime target for Communist attack. In some towns in Andalusia, which had been run by Anarchist councils since July, the introduction of governmental discipline touched off bloody rebellions. Thus the townspeople of Cullera, near Valencia, suddenly declared themselves independent, lit fires to attract Nationalist warships in the Mediterranean, and turned their guns on Valencia, now the provisional seat of the government. Republican troops were, in every case, dispatched to put down these local uprisings. Every such event gave further fuel to the Communist propaganda machine and further discredited the Anarchists.

In the Basque country an independent government, largely representing a coalition between moderate Socialists and middle-class Liberals, pursued its isolated way. In Catalonia still another semi-independent government gradually subdued the Anarchists by the simple expedient of involving them in government affairs. There, as elsewhere, the Communist party, on orders from Moscow, began a private war against its enemies on the left. The great Stalin purge trials had just commenced in Moscow, and their reverberations reached to Spain. "So far as Catalonia is concerned," the Russian newspaper *Pravda* cried, "the cleaning-up of Trotskyists and Anarchists has begun and it will be carried out with the same energy as in the USSR." The dreaded *NKVD,* the Russian secret police organization, with tentacles in Spain, operated with cold efficiency to eliminate those who opposed Communist policies. Fortunately for the government of Largo Caballero, these policies presently included all-out support of the government.

Opinion in the Republic continued to be divided as to what to do with property seized from Nationalist supporters and the great landlords of Andalusia. The Anarchists were in favor of immediate collectivization, while the Communists held that independent ownership would be more efficient for the present. Actually, the government collectivized certain areas but left the authority over the land in the hands of the local councils of peasants—who continued to work the land under much the same conditions as they had for centuries past.

The argument over what sort of army was needed for victory was resolved when Largo Caballero, at the urging of officers and Communists, abolished the independent militias. Henceforth the Republican Army was organized in mixed brigades—self-contained units with their own heavy weapons, artillery, medical, and supply services. Such units had first been organized by the Spanish Army during the Moroccan War. It was on this pattern that a Regular Republican Army emerged during the early part of 1937. The terrible lack of supplies continued to plague it, however. There were never enough rifles for training purposes; marksmanship was atrocious; there were few maps, no rangefinders, field glasses, or trench periscopes. Grenades blew up in the face of the thrower as often as they did in the face of the enemy.

Largo Caballero's government also halted the nationalization of foreign-owned companies. The seizure by workers of factories and mills was reversed wherever possible, and the peasant councils, which had held real power in the small towns and villages, were replaced by government administrators. This process of

Largo Caballero

slowing down and, indeed, reversing the revolution was carried
out with the full support of the Communists.

But when the political chaos of the Republic has been given its
full weight, it must never be forgotten that the Republican government, in the face of war, revolution, conspiracy, and the Communist stranglehold, was in fact trying to improve the lot of the
Spanish people. Five times as much money was spent on education
in Republican Spain during the first year of war as had been spent
in all of Spain in the last year of peace. The number of teachers
almost doubled, and thousands of schools were opened at the

front to teach 200,000 militiamen to read and write. On the land, too, in spite of its difficulties, the Republic moved forward. By May of 1937 nearly fifteen percent of the arable land of Spain had been turned over to the peasants who worked it. Tenant farmers dependent on the whims of absentee landlords became a thing of the past. Industrial production increased, despite the air raids, by forty percent. And the government's health program, despite the demands of the front, provided over a thousand new beds for tuberculosis victims. For the first time in Spanish history, compulsory inoculation against smallpox, diphtheria, and typhoid was inaugurated, and child welfare centers proliferated everywhere. In the great cities—Madrid, Barcelona, Valencia, Bilbao—as well as in the countryside, in spite of their agony, the people felt the thrill and excitement of what they hoped would be a new day. Where in the pages of history could be found a government that included an Anarchist Minister of Justice? This remarkable man, García Oliver, proclaimed, "When relations between men become what they should be there will be no need to steal and kill. For the first time let us admit here in Spain that the common criminal is not an enemy of society. He is more likely to be a victim of society. Who is there who says he dare not go out and steal if driven to it to feed his children and himself? . . . Justice, I firmly believe, is so subtle a thing that to interpret it one has need only of a heart."

The conditions in the two Spains at this moment were perhaps best exemplified by the confusion of Spanish intellectuals. Practically all of them had announced themselves in favor of the Republic at first. But after a few months of war many fled to foreign countries and there declared themselves neutral. One tragic victim of the confusion was Spain's great poet García Lorca, who was shot in the early days by Nationalists in Granada. Whether this murder was the result of a mistake, a private grudge, or Nationalist policy has never been conclusively established.

But the most dramatic intellectual and emotional confrontation between the two Spains was provided by the great Basque philosopher, Miguel de Unamuno. Formerly a Republican, Unamuno, as Rector of the University of Salamanca, found himself behind Nationalist lines when the Civil War burst out. He supported the Nationalists at first in their struggle for "civilization against tyranny," but was soon moved by Nationalist repression to change his views. On October 12, 1936, a day celebrated throughout the Spanish-speaking world in honor of Columbus and his followers, a great ceremony was held at the University. The Bishop of Salamanca was present, as was the Civil Governor and General Franco's wife, Señora Carmen Polo de Franco. Unamuno presided over the meeting.

After the opening speeches, General Millán Astray, the crippled founder of the Spanish Foreign Legion, arose and gave a violent harangue against the Catalan and Basque provinces. Referring to their separatist tendencies, he spoke of them as "cancers in the body of the nation. Fascism," he continued, "which is Spain's health-giver, will know how to exterminate both, cutting into the living healthy flesh like a resolute surgeon free from false sentimentality." One of Millán Astray's followers rose at the rear of the hall to shout out the Legion's battle cry, "Viva la Muerte!" (Long live death!). Immediately the General responded by leading the crowd in the Nationalist shout: "Spain! United! Spain! Great! Spain! Free!"

Slowly the aged Unamuno got up from his chair. He walked to the lectern and stared silently out over the crowd. Then he spoke, quietly, gravely.

"All of you are hanging on my words. You all know me and are aware that I am unable to remain silent. At times to remain silent is to lie. For silence can be interpreted as acquiescence. I want to comment on the speech—to give it that name—of General

Millán Astray, who is here among us. Let us waive the personal affront implied in the sudden outburst of vituperation against the Basques and Catalans. I was myself, of course, born in Bilbao. The Bishop here, whether he likes it or not, is a Catalan from Barcelona. Just now I heard a necrophilous and senseless cry: 'Long live death!' And I, who have spent my life shaping paradoxes which have aroused the uncomprehending anger of others, I must tell you, as an expert authority, that this outlandish paradox is repellent to me. General Millán Astray is a cripple. Let it be said without any slighting undertone. He is a war invalid. So was Cervantes. Unfortunately there are all too many cripples in Spain just now. And soon there will be even more of them if God does not come to our aid. It pains me to think that General Millán Astray should dictate the pattern of mass psychology. A cripple who lacks the spiritual greatness of a Cervantes is wont to seek ominous relief in causing multilation around him—"

At this point the enraged General Millán Astray shouted out, "Viva la Muerte!" again. His supporters in the crowd began to shout menacingly, but Unamuno continued relentlessly: "This is the temple of the intellect. And I am its high priest. It is you who profane its sacred precincts. You will win because you have more than enough brute force. But you will not convince. For to convince you need to persuade. And in order to persuade you would need what you lack: reason and right in the struggle. I consider it futile to exhort you to think of Spain. I have done."

There was a heavy silence. No words such as these had been publicly spoken in Nationalist Spain. Unamuno at that moment was in mortal danger of assassination by the Falangists present. But Señora Carmen Franco arose and, taking the elderly professor by the arm, accompanied him out of the hall, thus assuring his safety. Nevertheless this was Unamuno's last public appearance. He was placed under house arrest and passed his last months in broken-hearted contemplation of the disasters that had overwhelmed his beloved country.

VII

Three Famous Campaigns and One Infamous Failure

THE Nationalists opened the new year of 1937 with a well-planned campaign against the Republican-held city of Málaga. This city, with a population of nearly a hundred thousand, was the primary port and chief center of a long but narrow coastal strip reaching down the Andalusian coast almost to Gibraltar. Its capture, besides offsetting the moral effects of the Nationalist defeat at Madrid, was expected to provide a large Nationalist port on the Mediterranean for the reception of Italian supplies. Overall command of the Nationalist forces allotted for the conquest of this coastal plain was entrusted to Queipo de Llano, the man who had captured Seville single-handedly. Under him in field command was the Duke of Seville, a Bourbon prince.

Preparatory steps in the campaign were taken on January 17, when the Duke's forces, mainly from the Army of Africa, advanced from the south to seize the towns of Marbella and Torremolinos, in other years favorite resort cities for English tourists. Meanwhile troops from the garrison of Granada advanced under Colonel Antonio Muñoz to seize Alhama, north of Málaga. These events conveyed no warning to the Republican commander at Málaga, Colonel Villalba, that Málaga was threatened by full-scale attack. He was short of artillery, but the Republican government, now in Valencia, could not have sent him any, since the main Málaga-Valencia road running through the town of Motril was buried beneath floods. The Nationalists refrained from cutting Málaga off completely from Valencia only because the memory of desperate civilian resistance at Madrid made them hesitate to cut off escape routes.

The Republican forces in Málaga numbered some forty thousand—Andalusian militiamen, for the most part, who had not yet been affected by the Army reforms carried out elsewhere in the Republic. As always they were untrained and poorly armed. Colonel Villalba, a Regular Army officer, showed little resourcefulness and less confidence in the will of the population to resist. The city had been bombed regularly and shelled intermittently by sea so that it presented a desolate and ruined look even before the battle.

North of the city, Italian aid to the Nationalists had finally taken the ominous shape and form of nine highly mechanized battalions of Italian Blackshirts. Under the command of General Mario Roatta, former head of the Italian Military Intelligence and a devoted follower of Mussolini, these men wore special uniforms. They were kept under Italian command because *Il Duce* hoped that whatever glory they won in the subsequent battle would resound exclusively in Italy's honor.

On February 3, the main attack against Málaga began. Three battalions under the Duke of Seville advancing from Ronda in the south were held up by desperate resistance. But the next night, north of the city, the Italian forces, equipped with tanks, swung into action. Panic immediately enveloped the Republican militiamen—partly because of the awesome new tanks and partly because of Colonel Villalba's lack of spirit. By February 6, the Italians had reached hills that overlooked the main escape road north, and Villalba ordered a general evacuation of the city. Republican officers, political and trade union leaders—all fled up the coastal road, some on foot, some on bicycles. The fortunate few went in motor cars. Others made their way under cover of darkness to Valencia in small, coast-hugging fishing boats. The Nationalist cruisers *Canarias, Baleares,* and *Velasco* bombarded the town, while the German battleship *Graf Spee* stood nearby observing with interest. Republican fleet units that might have intervened were busily chasing phantoms in the form of Italian warships made to look like the *Canarias* and *Baleares.*

On February 8, just five days after the opening of the offensive, the Italians under Roatta and the Duke of Seville's battalions entered the ruined and abandoned city from north and south. Immediately, all those Republican sympathizers who had been unable to flee were rounded up. Many were shot at once on the beach, while others languished in prison only to be executed later after summary court-martials. The writer and philosopher Arthur Koestler, at that time a Communist propagandist, waited in prison for months under sentence of death and was only released in a chance exchange through the Red Cross for the wife of a Nationalist pilot.

Those who fled were little better off. Nationalist tanks and aircraft caught up with the long stream of Republican refugees on the road to Almería. Women and children were allowed to proceed (so as to increase the Republic's food difficulties), but many of the men were shot down in cold blood, often with their families watching.

Thus the Republic endured another defeat. And its causes were not glorious. If Villalba had inspired the citizens of Málaga and organized the kind of desperate resistance shown in Madrid, the city might have held out. If ill-trained Republican sailors' committees on their warships had not been so easily fooled they might have helped. If the Republican government at Valencia had rushed reinforcements, things might have been different. But the Thirteenth International Brigade, stationed nearby in Murcia, was not dispatched to save Málaga because the Communists feared that with its departure from the Valencia area, the Anarchists might seize the opportunity to rebel. The "ifs" of this badly managed campaign shook people's confidence in Largo Caballero's "Government of Victory."

While Nationalist forces thus seized all the southern Mediterranean coastal plain of Andalusia, the Nationalists on the Madrid front renewed their offensive. This was to take the form of a drive up the valley of the Jarama River in an attempt to cut the main Madrid-Valencia road. Five mobile brigades of the Army of Africa, powerfully supported by artillery and aircraft from the German Condor Legion, were assigned this task.

The Republicans had themselves been planning an offensive in the Jarama Valley. Republican Army divisions, under the command of General Sebastián Pozas, had been slowly moved into place and were still in many cases strung out along the roads leading to the front. The Nationalist blow that fell on February 6 caught both the Republican General and his troops completely by surprise. Driving rapidly north through the valley, the Nationalist forces overwhelmed the newly formed and largely disorganized Republican divisions and reached the junction of the Jarama and

Manzanares rivers by nightfall of February 7. The Republican retreat threatened to become a rout.

But on February 8, General Miaja, in command at Madrid, sent the crack Communist brigades under Enrique Lister and *El Campesino* along with elements from the Eleventh, Twelfth, and Fourteenth International Brigades to stiffen the Republican front. By February 9, the entire Republican defense had been reorganized. The troops dug themselves in on the heights overlooking the east bank of the Jarama River and awaited the Nationalist assault. They were unprepared for the form it took.

In the early hours of February 11, a group of Moroccan troops silently crept up to the approaches of the vital Pindoque Bridge, which spanned the Jarama. Making no sound, they slit the throats of the sentries (Frenchmen of the André Marty Battalion) one by one as they stood at their posts. Then, when the way was clear, they retired to their own lines. Immediately, two regiments of Nationalist cavalry thundered across the bridge. The startled Republicans on the other side blew up the mines they had previously planted, but the Pindoque Bridge, after rising a few feet into the air, settled back on its own foundations and thus gave the Nationalists a way across the Jarama. Meanwhile a second Nationalist force crossed the river some miles to the north. By three in the afternoon of February 11, the Nationalists had surrounded the main bulk of the confused André Marty Battalion. The Frenchmen fought until they were out of ammunition and most of them had been killed. Then the Moroccan cavalry charged and killed most of the survivors with knives.

By this time the Fifteenth International Brigade had been ordered into the line. A British battalion was assigned the task of defending what came to be known as "suicide hill." All night the men in the battalion dug themselves in and on the following day the main Nationalist blow fell upon them. For the first time,

Republican forces enjoyed air superiority. Russian-made fighter planes drove the German and Italian bombers from the sky. With their usual grim determination the British clung to "suicide hill," even after two-thirds of their men were killed or wounded. One of the British companies was tricked into capture by a Moroccan unit that advanced towards them singing "The Internationale." On February 13, the British finally retreated, but on orders from their commanding officers they turned right around and recaptured "suicide hill" in the face of severe Nationalist resistance. And that same day the Nationalists who had crossed the Jarama farther north were driven back to the banks of the river by the German battalions of the Eleventh International Brigade, led in the attack by Russian tanks under General Pavlov. On February 15, General Miaja himself took command of the front, organizing his Communist and International battalions into a firm line of resistance all along the river.

The International volunteers at this time were not all on the side of the Republicans. Whereas the miserable conscripts Mussolini had rounded up for his forces could hardly be called volunteers, a company of Irish men fighting on the Nationalist side were very definitely volunteers. Six hundred of these fought at Jarama, suffering heavy casualties.

On February 17, the Republican forces counterattacked. And this was the occasion when the American Abraham Lincoln Battalion of the Fifteenth International Brigade saw its baptism of fire. There were about five hundred men in the battalion at this time. All of them were young, most were students, many were merchant seamen. Their commander was Robert Merriman, a twenty-eight-year-old lecturer at the University of California. They fought with reckless courage and without artillery support. Over half the battalion was killed or wounded at Jarama. Years later, at battalion reunions, the survivors recalled that bitter fight to the tune of "Red River Valley":

There's a valley in Spain called Jarama.
It's a place that we all know so well,
For 'twas there that we gave of our manhood,
Where so many of our brave comrades fell.

127

We are proud of the Lincoln Battalion
And the fight for Madrid that it made.
So before we conclude this reunion,
Let us drink to our glorious dead.

The essential optimistic innocence of these men was captured by Ernest Hemingway in his article, "Spanish War," wherein he records a visit he made to a field hospital at the time. Comforting an American casualty, he was told by the wounded man, "They tell me Dos Passos and Sinclair Lewis are coming over too." "Yes," replied Hemingway, "and when they do I'll bring them up to see you." "Good boy, Ernest," the wounded man exclaimed. "You don't mind if I call you Ernest?" "Hell no!" replied Hemingway.

But while the armies with their foreign volunteer units distinguished themselves on both sides of the line for bravery and determination, a less heroic struggle was taking place in the foreign ministries of the world. Among the diplomats engaged in this softspoken war, lies took the place of bullets, cowardice was regarded as the sensible attitude, and appeasement was the order of the day. Early French support for the Spanish Republic had so frightened the British government that it issued an outright warning to Léon Blum, French Premier, to the effect that if France found herself at war with Germany over Spain, Britain would not feel bound to support her. From that moment on the French, although they continued secret aid to the Republic, worked night and day to get all the nations concerned by the Spanish war—Britain, Russia, Italy, and Germany—to sign a nonintervention agreement whereby each of them solemnly swore to refrain from sending arms or men to either side in Spain. The British welcomed this and signed immediately. The Russians and Italians and Germans, each for different reasons, but each with the determination not to live up to their signatures, signed soon after.

Thus, while the Germans, Italians, and Russians prepared to break their word, the British and French, under the leadership of Foreign Secretary Anthony Eden, called a meeting to establish a nonintervention committee that would take steps to make sure that the agreement was enforced. It met in London on September 9, 1936, and immediately degenerated into a debating society. The French accused the Italians of dispatching airplanes to Franco; the Italians accused the French of shipping guns to the Republic. Germany and Russia charged each other with various lies. Most of these accusations were, of course, true. All these nations except England continued to send men and arms to one side or the other. But to the British it was not so much the actuality of nonintervention that mattered as the appearance of it. With true British aplomb, the cabinet of Stanley Baldwin knew that as long as each country was not publicly committed to a victory of either side in Spain, there was little likelihood of general war breaking out. The French were forced to go along with English policy. The Germans and Italians and Russians were prepared to go along with any amount of talk—provided they remained free to intervene.

On March 8, 1937, an international board of control was established to administer actual control of nonintervention. Observers were to be posted on the French and Portuguese sides of the Spanish frontier, naval patrols were to establish watch over Spanish coasts, and international air control was to be instituted —all with the object of keeping foreign supplies and troops out of Spain. The protests of the Spanish Republic that as the legal government of Spain it was entitled under all international law to purchase arms abroad were ignored. The major powers feared a general war and were determined not to allow legal technicalities to stand in the way of their preventing it. The Germans and Italians agreed to participate in this control scheme because they planned to evade it and, in any case, thought they had already delivered enough arms to the Nationalists to ensure their victory. Russia agreed to participate because it brought her into closer association with France and England—the two powers she hoped to ally herself with in any war against Germany. The actual interests of the Spaniards on either side in Spain were always subordinated by the great powers to their own ends.

An example of the effectiveness of the Nonintervention Control Board occurred almost immediately. It was reported that organized Regular Army divisions of Italians were present at the battle of Guadalajara. Without bothering to deny the charges, Count Dino Grandi, the Italian representative on the control commission, said he hoped that none of the Italian "volunteers" would be withdrawn from Spain until the end of the war. In face of this flagrant betrayal of the Nonintervention Control Board's purposes the Russians and English and French confined themselves to a verbal protest—the Russians because they, too, were cheating, the British and French because they were simply frightened of provoking the Italians and Germans. The policy of appeasement, whereby Britain and France gave in time and again to the demands of Hitler and Mussolini in the hope of buying them off, was just getting firmly under way. Its more disastrous consequences were still in the future, but its shamefulness was apparent over Spain.

On the battle-torn fields of Spain, the struggle continued. If the battle of the Jarama had raised Republican morale (it was the first time the Nationalists had been defeated in open country), the results of the battle of Málaga encouraged the Italian generals on Franco's staff to think they might be able to encircle Madrid by driving down from the north upon the city of Guadalajara. For this purpose 20,000 legionnaires and Moroccans were organized under Colonel Moscardó, the hero of the Alcázar, while 30,000 Italians, divided into four divisions (the Black Flames, the Black Shirts, the Black Arrows, and the Littorio) and supported by 250 tanks and 180 pieces of mobile artillery, were assembled to burst through the Republican lines in *blitzkrieg* tactics. General Roatta, the Italian conqueror of Málaga, was in overall command. Mussolini took great personal interest in the coming offensive. He was sure it would prove to the world how efficient and aggressive the new Italian Army had become.

On March 8, 1937, the Nationalist offensive against Guadalajara began. Moscardó's forces and the Black Flame division broke through the disorganized Republican front and advanced rapidly all through the day and through the next two days. By March 10 they had reached the little city of Brihuega, barely fifteen miles from Guadalajara. The situation looked bad for the Republicans.

But by that date General Miaja had hastily thrown the Republic's best troops into the field. These included elements of Lister's regiment, the Eleventh International Brigade, a Basque brigade, *El Campesino's* brigade, and the Garibaldi Battalion of anti-Fascist Italians from the Twelfth International Brigade.

At noon on March 10, the Garibaldi Battalion, advancing up the road to Brihuega, encountered a patrol of the Italian Black Flame division. Thinking that any Italian-speaking troops they met must certainly be Nationalist, the Black Flame men advanced confidently—only to be cut to ribbons by machine gun fire from the Garibaldi Battalion. All afternoon the battle raged—an Italian Civil War fought out in miniature on the plains of central Spain. Meanwhile Count Galeazzo Ciano back in Rome was assuring the German ambassador that "our opponents are mainly Russians." The Garibaldi Battalion held up the Italian advance long enough for Republican bombers from nearby Barajas Airport to smash heavily at the mechanized columns. Then, led by General Pavlov's Russian tanks, the Republicans counterattacked and regained some of their lost ground. The Russian tanks raised havoc in the Nationalist lines. Had they been closely followed by infantry they might have broken through. But by

"The Italian character must be formed by fighting!" Italian prisoners captured by the Loyalists after Guadalajara.

this time the Garibaldi Battalion was too busy rounding up prisoners at bayonet point to give the tanks the support they needed.

On March 18 the entire Republican Army on the Guadalajara front, heavily reinforced and re-equipped, went over to the offensive. Republican planes pounded the Nationalists unmercifully as Pavlov's tanks roared into action—this time closely followed by masses of eager infantry. Although the Spanish Nationalists under Moscardó retreated in good order, by midday the Italian Army was enveloped in defeat. Entire divisions broke and ran. The roads were littered with rifles, grenades, equipment of all sorts that the fleeing troops had abandoned. The Italians were consumed in disaster. They lost over six thousand men and almost all their equipment. Hundreds of prisoners were taken by the pursuing Republicans.

Guadalajara was thus a stunning defeat for the Nationalists, but more especially for their Italian ally, Mussolini. He was enraged. Having conscripted men to fight a war they neither understood nor wanted, he now proclaimed that no Italians would be allowed to return home alive until they had won a great victory.

On the Republican side many foreign observers mistook the victory of Guadalajara as the decisive battle of the war. Actually, however, it had been a defensive success. The Nationalists, although they failed to complete the encirclement of Madrid, did retain a few miles of the territory they had won at the beginning of the campaign. But from this time on there were to be no major battles launched in the area around Madrid. Here the Republic was too strong.

An indication of the intensity of Spanish insular pride (and of the dislike aroused by Mussolini's men among *all* Spaniards) was given when the Falangist Fernández Cuesta, who was actually a Minister in General Franco's government, referred to the Italian disaster at Guadalajara as "the sole satisfaction I have experienced during the war."

VIII

The Basque Tragedy

WITH the possibility of a quick victory dead on the plains around Madrid, the Nationalists now turned their attention north. If the Republic was not to be overwhelmed by frontal assault, perhaps it could be defeated section by section. Because of the semi-independence achieved by the Basques, the lack of cooperation between them and the Republican government at Valencia, and, above all, because of the isolation of the Basque provinces from the rest of Republican Spain, the prospects for success in the north seemed good. Accordingly, on March 22, 1937, General Franco mapped out an offensive against the Basque provinces. For this purpose the Army of the North, under General Mola, was reorganized and re-equipped. The Italians, still smarting from their defeat at Guadalajara, were to join in this offensive, where they had better prospects of winning Mussolini's longed-for victory. All available airplanes and most of the Nationalist mobile artillery were placed at Mola's disposal.

The people against whom this new Nationalist blow was directed were an ancient race of mysterious origin. Long before the dawn of written history they had inhabited a small corner of Spain at the western edge of the Pyrenees Mountains, on the coast of the Bay of Biscay. They spoke a language of prehistoric origin that had no connection with Spanish, or for that matter, with any other spoken tongue. About one hundred thousand Basques lived in France; four hundred and fifty thousand lived in the Spanish provinces clustered around the great commercial port city of Bilbao. They were a hardy, devout, and shrewd people. Most Basques were farmers, though many followed the sea.

The city of Bilbao, third largest in Spain, had a large industrial working class. The Basque shrewdness in business and commerce (they had been often called the "Scots of Spain") was evidenced by the large and prosperous banks in Bilbao, by a large and comfortably established middle class in that city, and by the heavy trade carried on in normal years with England and the rest of the world. The Basques had never been conquered by the Moors and were particularly noted for their religious devotion. Catholicism in the Basque provinces, as in Ireland, was mixed with a streak of puritanical fervor that it did not always show in Latin countries. Above all, the Basques were noted for their fierce spirit of independence.

Since the reign of Ferdinand and Isabella the Basques had enjoyed, from time to time, political autonomy within the Spanish nation and had always fought to enforce respect for their civil liberties. Every two years, assemblies of all Basque men over the age of twenty-one would meet beneath an ancient oak tree in the

José Aguirre

town of Guernica. To this place the reigning Spanish king would send his representatives to swear before the Basque people his continued respect for Basque rights. A council of elders would then be elected to rule for the next two years. Over the centuries, this oak tree and the town of Guernica acquired a reverent, almost mystical significance in Basque minds as the center of their national life.

But in the nineteenth century, as the result of backing Don Carlos in the Carlist Wars, Basque rights were abolished by the monarchy. At the same time industrialization transformed the Basque center of Bilbao into a modern commercial city with a large, well educated, and overwhelmingly Socialist working class.

Left-wing political leaders, with the grievances peculiar to their following, thus found themselves in this small section of Spain in agreement with the rich and influential. All kept up a constant and growing demand for Basque home rule. The Basque agitation for self-government, unlike the similar movement in Catalonia, was always deeply religious. Thus, when the Republic had been established, and the *Cortes* met to consider those articles of the new Spanish constitution that would diminish the Church's influence in the nation, the Basque delegates walked out.

Nevertheless, the Republic restored to the Basques their ancient rights. Under the provisions of the Basque Statute, approved by a plebiscite in the Basque provinces and later confirmed by the Republican government's decree in Madrid, they achieved almost complete local autonomy. Socialists, Nationalists, Catholics, rich, poor—all Basques could unite behind their old battle cry: "For God and our old laws!"

They had chosen as president of their autonomous republic a young, conservative lawyer named José Aguirre. Under his leadership after the rebellion of July, 1936, a Basque Army of about fifty thousand men had been formed to defend the land against the Spanish Nationalists. The Basque Army was commanded by General Llano de la Encomienda, sent by the Republic after he had helped put down the Nationalist rising in Barcelona. The Army suffered from the usual Republican shortages. Many battalions had no machine guns at all; there were never enough rifles; the Basque Air Force consisted of forty obsolete planes; and there were only twenty-five tanks in the whole Army. But Basque industries were large and her industrial workers determined. They constructed a defensive line around the city of Bilbao that became known as the "Ring of Iron." This line was considered impregnable, but was intended only as a last-ditch defense. On the foothills of the Pyrenees, the Basque lookout posts watched—and waited.

Before he launched his armies to the attack, General Mola issued an ultimatum to the Basques. "I have decided," he declared, "to rapidly terminate the war in the north. Those not guilty of assassinations and who surrender their arms will have their lives spared. But, if submission is not immediate, I will raze all Vizcaya [the principal Basque province] to the ground, beginning with the industries of war."

That this was no idle threat was proved on March 31, 1937, when planes of the Condor Legion dive-bombed the defenseless country town of Durango, killing over two hundred civilians. That same day, under heavy artillery bombardment, the Nationalist offensive began. In the center of the front, heavy fighting took place around the town of Ochandiano. Outmaneuvered and threatened by flanking movements, constantly under air attack, the Basque lines slowly retreated. They were spared a disaster in the field only by the intervention of bad weather, which grounded Mola's planes at the beginning of April.

Meanwhile, behind the Basque fighting line, the problem of food for their towns and the great city of Bilbao became acute. Ever since the early days of the war Nationalist ships had imposed a loose blockade of the Basque ports. On April 6, 1937, the Nationalists announced to the world that henceforth a formal blockade of Bilbao existed and they would stop ships of any nationality from entering that port. On that day the British vessel *Thorpehall* was stopped by the Nationalist cruiser *Almirante Cervera*. But the hasty arrival of two British destroyers, H.M.S. *Blanche* and H.M.S. *Brazen*, persuaded the Nationalists to allow the steamer to pass.

Formal Nationalist blockade of Basque ports posed a very serious problem for the British government. On the one hand it was certainly legal for *belligerents* to proclaim a blockade of enemy ports during time of war. But, on the other hand, Stanley Baldwin and his cabinet had refused to recognize either side in Spain as belligerents. The reason for this technicality was that a large British trade (not, of course, involving arms), transported almost entirely in British ships, was carried on with the Spanish Republic. But the Nationalists held effective command of the seas. To recognize them as belligerents would automatically give them the right to interrupt this profitable British trade in any and all Spanish ports. The British government found a way out of this difficulty on the technical point of international law which states that a blockade, to be legal, must be effective. Thus, they could assume that the Nationalist blockade of Bilbao was effective without necessarily assuming the same for other Spanish ports. The Admiralty therefore obediently reported that Nationalist warships were in constant patrol off Bilbao and that the entrance to the port had been heavily mined. All British merchant vessels were warned to keep away from Basque waters—and the Admiralty declined to offer protection to any who disregarded this warning.

It was in a desperate attempt to prove to the world that the Nationalist blockade was not, in fact, effective that three small Basque trawlers put to sea to fight the Nationalist cruiser *Canarias* on February 26, 1937. The small trawlers fought until they were shot to pieces and two-thirds of their crews dead.

Nevertheless, by April, 1937, the British Admiralty had already warned all British shipping away from the Basque coast. Several British merchant ships found themselves, early in April, waiting in the French port of Saint Jean de Luz for Admiralty permission to carry food into Bilbao. Three of these ships happened to be commanded by Welsh captains, and each of the captains happened to be named Jones. For this reason they were distinguished by their cargoes as "Potato Jones," "Corn Cob Jones," and "Ham and Eggs Jones." But while these captains enjoyed interviews with the press and hinted that they might run the blockade at any moment with or without the help of the Royal Navy, another British ship slipped out of harbor. This was the merchant vessel *Seven Seas Spray,* under command of Captain W. H. Roberts.

Leaving Saint Jean de Luz at sunset on April 19, Captain Roberts refused to turn back when ordered to do so from shore. He also paid no attention to a warning he received from a British destroyer ten miles out of Bilbao. Instead, at eight o'clock the following morning, he ran his brave ship straight through the supposed Nationalist blockade, the mine fields, and the mist to enter Bilbao. As the *Seven Seas Spray* docked, the hungry people of Bilbao swarmed down to the pier to shout: "Long live the British sailors! Long live Liberty!"

Most important of all, however, the *Seven Seas Spray* forced the British Admiralty to admit that the Nationalist blockade of Bilbao was not, in fact, effective. This meant that British vessels making for that city had the right to protection from the Royal Navy in international waters. The British ships at Saint Jean de Luz immediately put this to the test. One of them, the *MacGregor,* while still ten miles out from Bilbao was ordered to stop by the Nationalist cruiser *Almirante Cervera.* The *MacGregor* sent off an S.O.S. to H.M.S. *Hood,* Britain's largest battleship, which was stationed nearby. The commander of the *Hood* requested the *Almirante Cervera* not to interfere with British ships in international waters. The captain of the *Almirante Cervera* replied that Spain's territorial waters extended six miles from the coast. The commander of the *Hood* answered that England recognized only a three-mile limit and ordered the *MacGregor* to proceed. The *MacGregor* did so, and just outside the three-mile limit, a Nationalist trawler, the *Galerna,* fired a warning shot across her bows. But a British destroyer, H.M.S. *Firedrake,* rushed up to order the *Galerna* not to attack a British ship. At this moment the Basque shore batteries let off a salvo at the *Galerna,* and she quickly left the scene of action. *MacGregor* sailed triumphantly into Bilbao, and from that time onward the Nationalists made no attempt to interfere with British trade to the Basques.

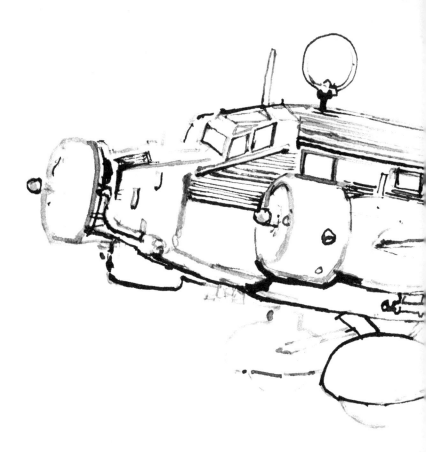

The relative calm of the fighting front was now broken by an event that was to sear the conscience of the world: the bombing of Guernica.

Guernica, with its ancient Basque oak and its traditions as the center of Basque national spirit, was, in actuality, a small market town situated about twenty-three miles behind the battle lines. On Monday, April 26, 1937—a market day when the town was crowded with farmers from miles around—the church bells of Guernica rang out at half-past four in the afternoon to announce the approach of enemy planes. A few minutes later Heinkel bombers, followed by Junker bombers, roared in over the town. After bombing it they turned to machine-gun the streets. Those who tried to run from the town were shot down on the roads by the Junkers. Both high explosive and incendiary bombs were dropped.

Wave after wave of bombers passed over every twenty minutes for three hours. The entire center of the city was destroyed, over 1,600 people were killed and close to a thousand wounded. Miraculously, the Basque oak escaped damage.

The news of this terrible raid upon a defenseless village was quickly carried around the world. Outraged protests from democratic governments poured into Nationalist headquarters. Although the Nationalists attempted to deny that there had been any raid (they claimed the Republicans had wrecked the city accidentally by blowing up a munitions dump), the evidence against them was overwhelming. A Nationalist staff officer was later heard to exclaim, "We bombed it and bombed it and bombed it and—well, why not?" The German pilots of the Condor Legion who had carried out the raid were later described as "sickened" by its results. But this was no use to the thousands of dead and dying amid the flaming wreckage. It now seems certain that the raid was coldly and deliberately planned (possibly without the knowledge of General Mola) by the German commanders of the Condor Legion as an experiment in mass-terror bombing—something the world of 1937 knew little about.

The bombing of Guernica, more than any single event of the Spanish Civil War, was to haunt the consciences of men everywhere. The great Spanish artist, Pablo Picasso, who had been commissioned by the Republic to paint a mural for the Spanish Pavilion at the Paris World's Fair, now began work on a painting, entitled "Guernica," which, showing the horrors of war, is often held to be his greatest masterpiece.

Two days after this raid both Guernica and Durango fell to to the Nationalists after a slight struggle. On April 30, the Italian Black Arrow division, still seeking glory for Mussolini, captured the fishing village of Bermeo. But there the luckless Italians soon found themselves surrounded and were reduced to begging for help from the other Nationalist forces. That same day the citizens of Bilbao were overjoyed to see the Nationalist battleship *España* sink outside their harbor after hitting a mine.

Having got used to air attack, the Basque militia stiffened their resistance and held their lines on all fronts. All through the month of May, 1937, Nationalist armies pounded at the Basques. While the Germans tried various bombing techniques (including the dropping of incendiaries into forests to burn out the defenders), the Republican government in Valencia tried desperately to send help. But Republican planes trying to reach the Basque provinces were often shot down over the large expanse of Nationalist territory they had to cross, while only a small amount of supplies passed the blockade. Republican officers, including the Russian General Ian Berzin, were sent to Bilbao in a vain effort to reorganize the Basque Army. But their efforts came too late; slowly but surely the Basques were being pushed back towards Bilbao and its famous "Ring of Iron." The Italians trapped at Bermeo were relieved by a Nationalist brigade.

The British and French governments, under heavy pressure from their people, were horrified by the attack on Guernica and now offered to provide ships and naval escort to carry Basque refugee children from the city of Bilbao. The Basques gratefully accepted this offer, and several thousand of their children were carried to safety in England and France. Some lived in homes, but most found themselves in special camps set up to receive them.

In a desperate attempt to draw the Nationalist armies from the Basque front, the Republic launched two offensives: one in Aragon and one south of Madrid. But, after some slight initial successes, both of these were stopped by the Nationalists who did not even have to draw reserves from the north to do so.

But the Nationalist commander, General Mola, was not to enjoy victory. For on June 3, while on a flight to Burgos, his airplane crashed into a mountain peak, and he was killed. Thus the last of Franco's co-conspirators in the Spanish high command met his death, leaving General Franco in sole effective control of the Nationalist movement.

On June 11, under the command of General Fidel Dávila, the Nationalists began a general offensive against the Basques. Heavy artillery bombardment, followed by tank attacks, broke the Basque defenses and forced the militiamen back into the "Ring of Iron" surrounding Bilbao. But even here they were to find no relief. For unknown to the Basque commanders, a traitor named Antonio Goicoechea had long since told the Nationalists where they would find the weakest point of this defense line.

On June 12, after an all-day artillery barrage, a selected Nationalist brigade assaulted the "Ring of Iron" at this weak point, broke through easily, and threatened the Basques with encirclement. Amid the shelling, the smoke, and the confusion the Basques had no choice. They abandoned the "Ring of Iron" and retreated into the city of Bilbao.

Now an anxious conference between the Basque government and its military staff took place. Could Bilbao be defended? Russian General Berzin, with memories of Madrid, thought that it could, provided the civilians threw themselves into the battle. Most Basque officers did not think Bilbao could be saved—and many hesitated to commit the city to the destruction and bloodshed that would inevitably ensue. At last the Basque government decided to defend the city, but to send the civilians away to Santander, a Republican city farther west along the coast. This abandonment of the city by its population undermined any possible resistance in advance. Soldiers do not fight well for empty boulevards. Nor was their morale improved when, on June 14, the Basque government itself fled to Santander.

On June 15, the hastily organized Basque defenses within the city were assaulted by waves of Nationalist troops. Twenty thousand Nationalist shells poured into Bilbao. Street fighting, in which individual houses, floors of houses, and sometimes single rooms became tactical objectives, raged through the suburbs. Attack and counterattack changed the line again and again— but always, in the end, the Nationalists advanced. By the evening of June 18, all Basque units had been ordered to evacuate the now ruined city. On June 19, Nationalist tank patrols scouted the center of Bilbao. Certain fifth columnists now emerged from hiding, hung out Monarchist flags, and shouted triumphantly. Into their midst suddenly burst a Republican tank. It dispersed the demonstrators, shot down their flags, and then scurried off on the road to Santander.

That same afternoon the triumphant Nationalists took control of Bilbao. But, remembering the massacre at Málaga, General Franco forbade large troop units to enter the city, thus preventing atrocities and shootings.

"For God and our old laws!" President Aguirre inspects
Basque troops on the Santander front.

The Nationalist victory at Bilbao now brought to a climax a bitter quarrel that had broken out in the Catholic Church throughout the world. There could be no doubt that the Basques, unlike the rest of Republican Spain, had been devoutly, almost fanatically Catholic nor that their priests had vigorously supported them. How then could the Nationalists claim they fought for Catholicism? Conservative Catholics the world over asserted that the Basque Church was heretical and that Basque priests had carried weapons and fought in the lines alongside their soldiers. But the Basque clergy stoutly denied that any of their priests had ever carried weapons or that they were in any way tainted by heresy.

In the United States, at this time, a poll taken among Catholics revealed that sixty percent of them believed the Basque priests. Not that this could have any effect; American neutrality was so strictly enforced that a plan for the reception of Basque children in the United States had to be dropped in the name of nonintervention.

The Pope and his advisors at the Vatican continued to believe what they were told by the Spanish hierarchy. Though they expressed themselves as opposed to some of the Nationalist excesses, and though the Pope had just issued his famous encyclical "With Burning Sorrow" against the Nazis in Germany, the official Church policy continued to uphold the Nationalist cause in Spain.

In a general persecution after their victory, the Nationalists imprisoned four hundred Basque priests and monks. Sixteen of these were executed.

After consolidating their victory at Bilbao, the Nationalists allowed their men a few weeks' rest before attacking Santander, the small port city to which the Basque government and the remnants of its Army had fled. New reinforcements, especially of planes and tanks, were sent to the Army of the North which now numbered 106 battalions besides the three Italian divisions.

This Army had over sixty batteries of artillery and, of course, the Condor Legion in air support.

Against this force the Republicans at Santander could muster only fifty thousand ill-armed militiamen, supported by fifty batteries of antiquated guns and a few ancient airplanes. Republican General Gamir Ulíbarri was in command. Those Basque units that fought under him did so without enthusiasm. They had been driven from their own provinces and demoralized by the collapse at Bilbao.

The campaign at Santander opened on August 14 and followed

a sadly familiar pattern. Artillery and air bombardment, followed by flanking maneuvers, drove the militiamen from position after position. The Italians reached the important town of Escudo on August 18. In Santander itself civilians prepared to flee—many in overloaded fishing boats. The soldiers despaired of success, and the Basque government and other Republican authorities prepared to evacuate themselves. By August 23, the bulk of the Basques on the Santander front had been trapped into the coastal village of Santona by the advancing Italians. While the Basque government in Santander fled by plane to France, the Basque commander at Santona surrendered his men to the Italians. Under the terms of the surrender agreement, the Italians guaranteed the lives of all Basque soldiers. They also promised that any Basques so wishing would be free to leave the country.

But as the Italians took over Santona, another Nationalist column entered and quickly subdued the city of Santander. It soon became apparent that the Italians had no intention of honoring their agreement with the Basques. Two British ships in Santona harbor (one of which was the *Seven Seas Spray*), waiting to take Basque refugees to France, were ordered away empty by the Italian authorities. As they steamed from port, their captains could see long lines of Basque prisoners being marched down the coastal road to Santander. There they were turned over to the Nationalists. Imprisonments and executions followed.

Mussolini, thrilled by this victory, telegraphed congratulations to his commanders. But, among the Italian officers and men, there was widespread disgust at the treachery their high command had practiced on the Basques.

The successful termination of the campaign in the Basque provinces now freed the entire Nationalist fleet for operations in the Mediterranean. It gained for General Franco's forces the huge industries of Bilbao and permitted them to unite their armies for offensives against the Catalans and the central Republican areas.

But beyond that it brought to an end the ancient tradition of Basque independence. Henceforth the Basque language was not to be taught in the schools; Basque leaders who failed to find refuge in France or who unwisely trusted the Italians were tried and executed by military court-martials; and all traces of Basque separatism were to be stamped out. A tiny but ancient and honorable freedom-loving people had been destroyed, and the world, as well as Spain, was the poorer for it.

IX

Heroics, Chaos, and Stalemate

WHILE the Basques demonstrated their heroism to an admiring world, a group of Nationalists were exhibiting the same quality deep within Republican territory. High in the mountains of the Sierra Morena, on the borders of Andalusia and Castile, a small group of *Guardia Civil* with their families and supporters had held out for the Nationalist cause ever since the July uprising. The defenders, 250 *Guardia Civil,* 100 Falangists, and about 1,000 middle-class citizens of the town of Andujar, had dug themselves in on two mountain peaks around the Catholic shrine of Santa María de la Cabeza. During the first nine months of the war, the surrounding Republicans made no attack on this enclave

deep within their territory. But after several months of preparation, especially the gathering of food supplies, the Nationalists of
Santa María de la Cabeza decided it was their moral duty to let
the Republicans around them know how they felt. Therefore they
sent a messenger with a declaration of war against the Republicans.
They were immediately besieged by Republican militia. The leader
of the Nationalists was a captain of the *Guardia Civil,* Santiago
Cortés, whose wife and family were prisoners of the Republic in
the town of Jaén.

During the early days of the siege, the Nationalists at Santa
María de la Cabeza communicated with Nationalists in Cordova
and Seville by means of carrier pigeons. Nationalist pilots, spe-
cially trained in the techniques of dive bombing, dropped supplies
onto the tiny defense area. Since parachute drops were too likely
to be blown into the surrounding Republican territory, such deli-
cate appliances as medical instruments were dropped by turkey—
a bird whose flight pattern is almost vertical. Within the mountain
fortress, schools and hospitals were improvised, while outside ten
thousand Republican militia awaited the signal to attack.

"... they sent a messenger with a declaration of war."
Guardia Civil *firing from a roadside against Republican militia.*

THE CIVIL WAR IN SPAIN

At the beginning of April the Republican government decided to liquidate this island of nationalism and for that purpose sent the Thirteenth International Brigade to lead the assault. After a few days of bitter fighting on the steep slopes of the mountains, the Nationalist force was cut in two. The smaller area of resistance, known as Lugar Nuevo, sent its last carrier pigeon to Captain Cortés to inform him that they could no longer hold out. But, just as they were preparing to surrender, a wild and torrential downpour of rain began. Under cover of this storm, the Nationalists at Lugar Nuevo were transferred without loss into the sanctuary of Santa María de la Cabeza. By this time General Franco had sent orders to Captain Cortés giving him permission to surrender when resistance became impossible. He also ordered that the women and children among the defenders should be evacuated under guarantee of Red Cross officials. But Captain Cortés and his followers had little confidence in the ability of the Red Cross to carry out any such promises. They were surrounded by twenty thousand militiamen of doubtful discipline. Perhaps believing their own propaganda about the ferocity of their enemies, the Nationalists of Santa María de la Cabeza hesitated to surrender. The decision was made for them on April 30. On that day, following air and artillery bombardment, the International Brigade and the militia stormed up the mountain. Captain Cortés was wounded. By May 1, the Republicans had broken into the sanctuary itself. At first, amid the confusion, a general slaughter of the defenders took place. Santa María de la Cabeza was burned. But, while flames leaped from the mountain peak, most of the women and children were taken away by trucks and the rest of the defenders made prisoner. A few days later Captain Cortés died in a Republican hospital of his wounds, after leading a defense in every way worthy of the great Spanish *conquistador* whose name he bore.

While the Basques collapsed and Captain Cortés waged his

struggle in the mountains, a severe political crisis gripped the Republican government at Valencia. This was primarily due to the Communists' determination to oust Largo Caballero from his position as premier and to break up, if they could, the political organizations of their enemies on the left—the Anarchists and Trotskyists. The Communists now, for the first time, felt strong enough to undertake these measures. After all, was it not largely the determination of the Communists that had saved Madrid? Was it not Russia that supplied most of the arms and munitions to the Republic? Above all, it could not be denied that the Communists followed a policy of "win the war first, then talk about revolution." And this policy brought them the support of Liberals and most Socialists, as well as the military commanders. Besides, with advisors in Spain from all the leading Communist parties of the world, the Communists were undoubtedly led by men of very high ability. Largo Caballero and several of his cabinet members were already very jealous of the influence and prestige wielded by those Communist leaders such as *La Pasionaria* who had stayed behind to defend Madrid after the government fled. But, before the Communists could take conclusive steps to depose Largo Caballero, an unexpected crisis broke out in Barcelona.

In that great port city, ever since the beginning of the war the semi-independent government of Luis Companys had maintained itself in power by an uneasy coalition of Liberal, Socialist, Communist, Trotskyist, and Anarchist parties. While Communist influence in the city rose steadily, the Anarchists and Trotskyists grew desperate. Although they represented a large, even a majority section of the workers and peasants of Catalonia, their organizations and tactics constantly lost ground. When the government of Companys decided to reorganize the Barcelona police force so that private political affiliations would no longer dominate it, the Anarchists walked out of the cabinet. A new government, formed in April, 1937, failed to relieve the mounting tensions

*"Barcelona's private armies gathered . . ." An armed Anarchist directs
nervous pedestrians during the riots in Barcelona of May, 1937.*

within the city. Anarchist leaders in the Republican government
at Valencia urged their followers in Barcelona to moderation—
but in so doing only lost their influence among these followers.

On April 25, the Anarchist newspaper in Barcelona, *Solidaridad
Obrera,* published a violent attack on the Communists. This was
nothing new—but that same day a leading member of the Communist youth organization was murdered on the street, probably
by Anarchists. Local Communists, imagining these events to pres-
age a general attack, retaliated by shooting an Anarchist. All political parties now began to issue guns to their followers. Barcelona's
private armies gathered. Barricades appeared on some streets, and

various buildings were fortified. May 1, the traditional workers' holiday, was a silent and expectant day in Barcelona; the workers, instead of celebrating, were preparing to slaughter each other. The fighting started over a ridiculous mistake.

On May 2, Indalecio Prieto, a Socialist minister in Largo Caballero's cabinet, telephoned from Valencia. He asked to be connected to the Catalan government. The telephone exchange in Barcelona had long been staffed and run by the Anarchists. An Anarchist telephone operator at the Barcelona exchange replied that there was no such thing as a Catalan government—only councils of workers and peasants. This incident made the Catalan government decide to investigate matters. Accordingly, on May 3, a government inspection party arrived at the exchange and visited the censor's department on the first floor. But the Anarchist workers on the floors above, aroused from their midday *siesta,* imagined that the government had sent forces to take over the entire exchange and oust them. They immediately opened fire down the stairs on the inspectors below. Anti-riot troopers and police quickly appeared on the streets surrounding the building. Finally, convinced that they had been mistaken, the Anarchists within were persuaded to give up their arms. On the following day Anarchist leaders called on the Catalan government to remove the police stationed in the telephone exchange. But although the government promised to comply, by the evening of May 4 rifle fire was breaking out all over Barcelona.

As street fighting became widespread, the government and their supporters—including the Communists, the anti-riot troops, and the police—controlled about half the city, while the Anarchists and Trotskyists held the other half and most of the suburbs. The Ramblas, Barcelona's tree-shaded central thoroughfare, became the battle line. The scenes of July 19, 1936, were repeated. Rifle and machine gun fire swept the streets; passing cars were blown up by grenades dropped from the roofs of buildings. For five days Barcelona fought out its own private civil war. Attack and counterattack swept through the districts of the Catalan capital.

Meanwhile the Republican government in Valencia made frantic efforts to bring peace to the strife-torn city. Anarchist leaders there were generally successful in persuading their followers throughout the rest of Spain to keep the peace, but in Barcelona itself political truces and maneuverings alike went unheeded as more and more blood was spilled. On May 6, for example, while government police were assaulting Anarchist headquarters, a group of Anarchist youths dragged a 75mm artillery piece into position outside a cinema and then opened deadly fire on anti-riot troops watching the show within. But, by evening of that same day, two Republican cruisers and the battleship *Jaime Primero* arrived in Barcelona harbor with government troops and police from Valencia. These forces quickly restored order in the city, and by May 8 the riots were ended—at a cost of four hundred dead and over one thousand wounded. Although the fighting brought victory to neither side, it convinced many independent Republicans that the Communists at least stood for law and order, while the Anarchists and Trotskyists could not be trusted. It also provided the Communists with an excellent springboard for their attack on Largo Caballero.

Communist political leaders now hastened to denounce Caballero's government for having failed to foresee the Barcelona riots and for failing to take effective action to put them down. In Valencia, at a cabinet meeting, Communist ministers demanded that Largo Caballero disband the Trotskyist organization of workers (they did not feel quite strong enough to make a similar demand regarding the Anarchists) and arrest its leaders. Caballero, although a member of neither of these groups, replied (as the Communists had known he would) that as a worker he could not possibly break up any workers' organization. Thereupon,

Juan Negrín

many members of his cabinet, both Communist and non-Communist, offered their resignations. The following day Caballero had no choice but to present his own resignation to President Azaña. After a few days of confused maneuvering, Azaña in turn asked Juan Negrín to form a new government.

Negrín, who had the support of the Communists and Socialists, was almost unknown outside of Spain at this time. A former professor of physiology at the University of Madrid, he had joined the Socialist party during the last days of Primo de Rivera, and had been a deputy to the *Cortes* under the Republic. In September, 1936, Caballero had made him Minister of Finance, a post that he filled with energy and success. Largely because he had no great personal following, he was considered to be an excellent choice as a compromise premier. But if those around him thought he would be easily influenced, they were wrong. He soon revealed a strong and dominating temperament, which, along with very great intelligence, was to carry him safely through all the plots, intrigues, and maneuvers of his political allies, as well as the battles of war in the coming years. Mildly Socialist, he was ruthlessly opportunistic. He was prepared to make any sort of political "deal" that would help to win the war. But if this forced him to rely heavily on the Communists and on Russian support, it by no means made him a captive of Soviet policy. The Communists were to find Negrín a much tougher character than they had at first suspected. Under his rule, Communist influence was eventually to decline.

Negrín quickly formed a new cabinet, which, while it included the Socialist Indalecio Prieto as Minister of War, and two Communists, did not include any of the followers of Largo Caballero. When Negrín asked the Anarchists to join his government as they had that of his predecessor, they refused.

The new government was faced almost immediately by an international crisis. German fleet units, although they had taken no direct part in the war thus far, had certainly been giving aid and comfort to the Nationalists and, by their very presence, intimidating Republicans. During the first week of May, the German battleship *Deutschland* lay at anchor off the harbor of Nationalist-held Ibiza in the Balearic Islands. On May 26, just at sunset, two Republican planes swooped in over the harbor and dropped two bombs on the ship. Thirty-two German seamen were killed and nearly a hundred wounded. The attack was perfectly legitimate, Ibiza being a war harbor. But the choice of objectives was, to say the least, unwise. Although the matter was never satisfactorily cleared up, it seems probable that the bombing was due to lack of Air Force discipline rather than to government orders. In any event, the Republic disclaimed responsibility for the incident. But its denials rang false.

Hitler flew into one of his great rages when he heard of the attack. While the *Deutschland* sailed to Gibraltar to disembark her wounded, the German dictator plotted a suitable revenge. This was not slow in coming. On May 31, a German cruiser and four destroyers appeared off the Republican city of Almería, just down the coast from Valencia. They fired two hundred salvos into the city, killing nineteen people and wrecking many buildings before withdrawing.

At a hastily called cabinet meeting, Indalecio Prieto urged that the entire German fleet in the Mediterranean be bombed. True, this might start a world war. But perhaps that was the only way in which the democracies could be made to stand up to the Germans and Italians. Perhaps it would save the Republic. Premier Negrín, horrified by this plan and the support it received from other ministers, gained time by persuading the cabinet to await advice from President Azaña. The Communist ministers hurried to report matters to the party's central committee. The leaders went into hysteria and radioed to Moscow for instructions. Stalin replied that the Soviet government had no desire at all for world war. He advised that Prieto's plan had to be defeated—even if this meant the murder of Prieto himself. But by this time Negrín and Azaña had persuaded the cabinet not to start a war with Germany. In such a war, after all, could they realistically count on support from France and England? Not at a time when both those countries were outdoing each other in trying to appease the dictators. Besides, even to idealistic Spaniards, one war was enough.

In any event, the Republican government had more important things to consider—among them, a new and heavy offensive against the Nationalists on the Madrid front. Planned by General Miaja and the Communists, it was hoped that this offensive, by striking west of Madrid and towards the south, would cut off all the Nationalists still besieging the capital. An army of fifty

THE CIVIL WAR IN SPAIN

thousand men under the command of Miaja was assembled for this blow. Among its divisional and regimental commanders were to be found such famous names as Lister, Modesto, Jurado, and *El Campesino*. Units of the Eleventh, Thirteenth, and Fifteenth International Brigades were to fight shoulder to shoulder with famous Republican regiments. The offensive was to be supported by 150 planes, over 125 tanks, and more than 135 pieces of artillery. Its first objective was the tiny village of Brunete, almost due west of Madrid.

Among the International Battalions to fight at Brunete would be the Abraham Lincoln Battalion, still commanded by Robert Merriman, and the newly formed George Washington Battalion, commanded by Oliver Law, a Negro. For the Americans of these two battalions, Brunete was to prove a hell on earth. They, along with other units of the Fifteenth Brigade, were used as shock troops in the advance. Although they were decently armed and equipped, this bitterly fought battle was to be, for many of these volunteers, their last. In later years the survivors mockingly sang:

It was there on the plains of Brunete,
'Midst a hail of steel confetti;
With our planes and our tanks
We would break Franco's ranks;
All sick on Italian spaghetti!

At the time, however, there was little singing and no mockery. So many Americans were killed at Brunete (including Oliver Law) that their two battalions had later to be merged into one.

The Republican offensive broke over the front at dawn on July 6, 1937. Artillery and air bombardment caught the weak Nationalist divisions there by complete surprise. Within a few hours Nationalist lines had been broken, and the Republicans advanced to surround and then capture their first objective, Brunete.

As soon as they were aware of what was afoot, the Nationalists hurried to bolster their sagging lines. General José Varela was placed in command. Units of the Army of the South as well as the Condor Legion and heavy artillery from the north were rushed to support him. Within the space of thirty-one hours, thirty-one battalions of infantry and nine batteries of artillery arrived to support the Nationalist defense.

The Republican advance beyond Brunete was slowed by its own success. Having punched a narrow hole through the Nationalist lines, Republican commanders now tried to push as many battalions through it as they could. Wild confusion resulted. Eighty tanks, for example, made a disorganized and unsuccessful assault on the Nationalist-held village of Villafranca, without infantry support. By midnight on the first day of battle, General Varela was able to report to Franco that the front had been reestablished.

On July 9, in a new advance, *El Campesino's* brigade captured the town of Quijorna. Villafranca fell to other Republican units on July 11. By that time the battle—a raging storm of shells, tanks, planes, and sudden death, all sweeping over a parched earth in the intense heat of July—had become the bloodiest of the war thus far. On July 15 the Republicans were ordered to dig in where they stood to defend against the expected Nationalist counterattack. For three days the front remained quiet.

On July 18, the Nationalist blow fell on the Republican flanks. For a week the armies remained locked in a death grip of bayonet charges and screaming bullets. But by July 24 the Nationalists had finally broken through the Republican lines and recaptured the town of Brunete. General Varela, elated by this success, wanted to continue the attack right up to the gates of Madrid, but General Franco's caution prevailed, and the front was stabilized.

Thus, at a cost of 25,000 men killed, 100 aircraft lost, and mountains of precious war matériel expended, the Republic had gained an area of about thirty square miles west of Madrid. The Nationalist defense cost them 10,000 men and the loss of 23 airplanes. In spite of the small Republican advance, in terms of men and matériel, the battle of Brunete must be considered ultimately as a Republican defeat.

While the combatants recoiled in exhaustion from this bloody battle, events in the Mediterranean sea directed the world's attention once again to the successful game of bluff Mussolini was playing against England and France. The Italians had long since made the Nationalist Balearic Islands, especially the port city

". . . Nationalists had finally broken through the Republican lines . . ."
One of General Varela's Moorish guards watches Republican prisoners tied each to the other, after Brunete.

of Palma de Mallorca, their main base for aircraft and naval vessels. From there they were supposed to patrol the sea along with other members of the Nonintervention Control Board to ensure that no arms were shipped to either side in Spain. Actually they used the base to ship their own arms to Franco, to bomb Barcelona from time to time, and to refuel their ships, which blockaded part of the Republican coast. Now, stimulated by Nationalist reports of heavy Russian arms shipments to the Republic, Mussolini unleashed unrestricted submarine warfare in what he was pleased to call "Mare Nostrum" (Our Sea). During July and August, 1937, British, French, Spanish, Russian, and Danish vessels were torpedoed. The attacks were always ascribed to "unknown" submarines, and the British Admiralty seemed reluctant to try to find out their identity. But when H.M.S. *Havock,* a British destroyer, was attacked, it replied with depth charges, and the Admiralty had no difficulty in identifying the submarines as Italian.

The French government was in favor of (and prepared for) an immediate preventive war against both Italy and the Spanish Nationalists if these attacks continued. But the newly installed British government of Neville Chamberlain was determined to follow a policy of appeasement. Therefore another in the long and futile series of international conferences was called. All Mediterranean powers plus Russia and Germany were invited to attend. The Italians declined. Count Ciano, Italian Foreign Minister, wrote in his diary: "The full orchestra, the theme: piracy in the Mediterranean. Guilty—the Fascists. The Duce is very calm."

The conference, however, produced a strong plan for naval patrols. In the future, unidentified submarines that attacked merchant vessels were to be themselves attacked by patrol craft. Then, in a masterpiece of foolishness, the Italians were not only persuaded to join in the patrols but assigned the seas between Italy, Sardinia, and the Balearic Islands—thus enabling them to continue sending supplies to Franco without observation. Ciano now laughingly referred to himself as the "pirate turned policeman." Nevertheless, submarine activity was, for the present, curtailed.

As autumn advanced into the bitter winter of 1937–1938, the Republic planned yet another grand offensive to destroy Nationalist power. The attack was to be launched on the town of Teruel— partly because it was thought an easy objective, partly because it would threaten the Nationalist city of Saragossa. For political reasons no International Brigades were to be used at Teruel; the re-formed Republican Army was to accomplish this task as a demonstration of what it could do by itself. Under the command of General Hernández Sarabia, an army of 100,000 men was gathered for the assault.

Teruel itself was a dismal town of about twenty thousand inhabitants. It was famous for two things only—the lowest temperatures in Spain and the legend of the lovers of Teruel, a gloomy tale of jealousy and death.

On December 15, 1937, during a driving snowstorm, the Republican advance began without air or artillery bombardment. Two columns surrounded the town of Teruel and met on a mountainous ridge known as La Muela de Teruel to the west of the city. The Nationalist commander at Teruel, Colonel Rey D'Harcourt, drew his forces into the town and prepared for a siege. On Christmas Eve the Republican radio announced the fall of Teruel. But, although the Republican militiamen had penetrated the city, they had not yet captured it. Colonel D'Harcourt and his men continued to resist in bitter street fighting. On December 29, the Colonel received a telegram from General Franco instructing him to "trust in Spain as Spain trusts in you." Of more help to the beleaguered Nationalists, however, was the opening of a Nationalist counterattack that day to relieve them.

Generals José Varela and Antonio Aranda, in command of

Spain, October, 1937 (Shaded areas indicate Nationalist regions)

the Nationalist troops from Castile and Galicia, began their advance after heavy artillery bombardment. They were supported by the ever-faithful Condor Legion in the air. Although Republican lines were pushed back, they did not break. On New Year's Eve, the Nationalist forces reached La Muela de Teruel in atrocious weather. The Republicans resisted until snow, fog, and sleet reduced visibility to zero. Now, all along the front, roads were blocked by snowdrifts and the intricate engines of war froze to a standstill. Temperatures fell to eighteen degrees below zero. If both armies suffered from the cold, undoubtedly the Moroccan troops on the Nationalist side, unprepared for severe winters, suffered most. On both sides frostbite became the enemy. Limbs were amputated by the hundred. A four-day blizzard left six hundred trucks snowbound on the Republican supply road from Valencia.

Meanwhile Colonel D'Harcourt's men fought on within the city. Savage house-to-house and hand-to-hand combats forced him into a smaller and smaller section of the town. Without medicine, food, or supplies and with little water, the Nationalist defenders fought now among piles of ruins. On January 8, 1938, D'Harcourt surrendered. Immediately he and his men and all civilians in the city were evacuated behind Republican lines. And now the Republicans dug in at Teruel to withstand a siege by the Nationalists.

After a two-week pause to strengthen and reinforce their troops, the Nationalists renewed their attack. While Russian, German, and Italian planes fought it out in the skies above the city, heavy artillery roared at the Republican lines. On January 17 these lines broke. A general Republican defeat was only prevented at the last moment by the arrival of the International Brigades in the front lines. Nevertheless the Nationalists captured La Muela de Teruel.

On January 27 the Nationalist advance was held by Republican counterattacks. But while the militiamen were holding at

Teruel, the Army of Africa, under command of General Yagüe, made a decisive advance north of the city. In a sudden and savage assault on this lightly held Republican front, Yagüe's men swept forward to a victory that, by February 7, had gained nearly seven hundred and fifty square miles of Republican territory, seven thousand prisoners, and vast military booty.

On February 17, 1938, the Nationalists launched their final drive on Teruel. Yagüe, sweeping down from the north, threatened the town with encirclement. Other Nationalist forces, attacking from the south, threatened to cut the Republican supply line at Valencia. On February 20, the Republicans were forced to abandon the town. They left ten thousand men dead and fourteen thousand prisoners, besides much war matériel. The front at Teruel, like the fronts at Guadalajara and Brunete, now lapsed into stalemate.

Thus, as the fateful year of 1938 dawned upon an apprehensive world, the Spanish Civil War had almost completely lost its first amateurishly enthusiastic appearance. Battles now were fought, not with half-trained militiamen, but with disciplined army divisions. Battles in which neither side seemed able to gain a decisive advantage now recorded casualties numbered in tens of thousands. If both sides now showed more respect for the fighting abilities of their opponents, neither side showed any inclination to seek peace. Instead, Spain settled into the long and bloody agony of a war of attrition.

X

Journal of a War: March– November, 1938

MARCH 1—Communist party opens one of its deadly campaigns of political assassination against Indalecio Prieto, Negrín's Socialist Minister of War. Led by *La Pasionaria,* Communists begin denouncing Prieto for "defeatism." Negrín holds his government together only with the greatest difficulty. General Franco prepares another offensive, this time to be directed against the northern front in Aragon. Objective: Barcelona and the extinction of the Catalan government. General Fidel Dávila is given command of Nationalist forces on this front with Colonel Ituarte Moscardó and General Juan de Yagüe under him. Italian divisions are to be used as well as the indispensable Condor Legion.

March 5–6—The Nationalist cruisers *Baleares, Canarias,* and *Almirante Cervera* are attacked off Cartagena by Republican cruisers *Libertad, Mendez Múñez,* and four destroyers. In wild fighting, the destroyers torpedo and sink the *Baleares.* All Spanish ships then flee the scene of action. British destroyers are bombed by Republican planes while picking up survivors of *Baleares.* The Nationalist admiral goes down with his ship.

March 9—The Nationalist offensive in Aragon opens with a terrific artillery barrage and heavy aerial bombardment. Republican troops are exhausted after their fighting at Teruel. Their war supplies are very low. Many men have been seen entering the front lines without rifles. Their lines are broken, and Yagüe starts rolling down the right bank of the river Ebro against almost no resistance.

March 10—The Nationalist Army seizes the key town of Belchite in Aragon. Men of the Fifteenth International Brigade are the last Republican troops to flee the town. Merriman, commanding American battalions, is killed today. Italian divisions are held briefly by heavy fighting at Rudilla. Black Arrows break through the line. In Rome, Count Ciano is jubilant. Republican units are retreating at top speed all along the front.

March 11—A new Nationalist *Falange* labor law announced. By its terms hours and conditions of work are to be regulated and a minimum wage guaranteed; social insurance and family allowances, as well as paid vacations, are to be granted. Peasants are to be allowed enough land to meet their family needs. Tenant farmers are to be protected against eviction. Labor unions are to be replaced by syndicates controlled by the state, eventually merging into the government structure. Most of these aims will not be realized for many years.

March 15—The collapse of the Republican front in Aragon causes Premier Negrín to fly to Paris to beg Léon Blum's government to open the French frontier to shipments of arms. The

French, horrified by Nationalist success, propose everything from war against Italy to the dispatch of a French mechanized division to aid the Republic. But pressure from Britain forces them to do no more than open the frontier. Blum and Negrín watch the first arms shipment pass through on March 17.

March 16–19—Barcelona is heavily bombed by Italian planes based in Palma de Mallorca. Beginning at ten o'clock in the evening, waves of planes drop high explosives on the city every three hours. By three o'clock on the following afternoon, 1,300 people are dead and over 2,000 wounded. Ciano in Rome remarks that General Franco was not informed of these raids that were ordered personally by Mussolini. France is enraged by the bombings and demands they be stopped at once. The people of Barcelona are not frightened—only infuriated by this mass attack. Protests pour in from democratic governments around the world, without effect.

March 20—The Nationalist advance in Aragon continues. The town of Caspe falls after a heroic defense by the Fifteenth International Brigade. The Nationalists have now advanced sixty miles on a broad front since the offensive began. Nationalist troops are given a rest while regrouping for the next attack.

March 22–25—The Nationalist offensive is resumed. General Ituarte Moscardó's men blast the Republicans on a hundred-mile front, forcing them to abandon their positions before Saragossa. Yagüe crosses the river Ebro and advances swiftly. The Aragonese villages are captured one after another. Republican refugees from these towns clog the roads leading to Barcelona. They are machine-gunned from the air. Yagüe, advancing now into Catalonia itself, is held up for one week at Lérida by a desperate defense conducted by *El Campesino*. To the north, Nationalist columns are pinned down in the foothills of the Pyrenees. Isolated among the valleys, their columns make good targets for Republican air attack. In the south, Nationalist forces drive without resistance towards the Mediterránean Coast. Individual Republican units fight heroically, but a front no longer exists. German and Italian air strategists are using their planes like cavalry to drive Republican units from hastily fortified positions. While Spanish blood stains the fields of Aragon, German and Russian observers learn much about the use of planes in close infantry support.

March 26—Juan Negrín returns from Paris. He finds Barcelona engulfed in gloom. Apparently Communist charges are correct. War Minister Indalecio Prieto is the source of much of this despair; he has become a confirmed defeatist. Prieto wants to make a negotiated peace with the Nationalists and has made several efforts to contact Nationalist agents, but with no success. Negrín calls a cabinet meeting to be presided over by President Azaña. At this crisis meeting he proposes to remove Prieto as Minister of War but keep him in the cabinet. Prieto still has many loyal followers among the Socialists. While the ministers debate in the Pedralbes Palace, a huge Communist-led mob, carrying banners and placards on which such slogans as "Down with the Minister of War!" are written, surges against the palace gates. From the street below Prieto can hear *La Pasionaria* denouncing him to the crowd. Negrín persuades the mob to disperse after promising the people a more forceful prosecution of the war.

March 28—*El Campesino* carries on at Lérida against heavy Nationalist pressure. The Fifteenth International Brigade is holding the enemy at the town of Gandesa. At a meeting of the War Council in Barcelona, Prieto succeeds in demoralizing all present by his gloomy predictions of defeat.

March 29—Negrín ousts Prieto as War Minister. Opponents charge Negrín with bowing to Communist pressure over Prieto. But there is no doubt that Prieto is, in fact, a defeatist. There is also no doubt that Russian military supplies are now pouring into the Republic by way of the open French frontier. If Negrín is not to cooperate with the Communists, with whom is he to cooperate?

THE CIVIL WAR IN SPAIN

Prieto leaves the government, blaming Communist interference in the conduct of the war. But he cannot offer any alternative to cooperation with the Russians. His own hopes for a negotiated peace have failed because Franco will accept only unconditional surrender. The Republic apparently has no choice but to continue the struggle—with Soviet arms.

April 3—Lérida and Gandesa both fall to the Nationalists. In Gandesa 140 British and Americans are made prisoners. The heroic defense of these two towns has, however, gained a week of valuable time for the Republic. The southern column of the Nationalist Army, under command of General Antonio Aranda, has driven to within sight of the Mediterranean sea. It is held up by stiff resistance at Tortosa. Should this column reach the sea, the Republic will be cut in two.

April 8—The Nationalists fighting in the Pyrenees capture the towns of Tremp and Camarasa. Thus, Barcelona is cut off from her electric power sources on the river Ebro. Henceforth electricity in Barcelona is supplied by the city's ancient steam generating plants.

April 15—Nationalist troops, under the command of General Vega, capture the fishing village of Vinaroz. The Nationalist soldiers run triumphantly into the sea while their general makes the sign of the cross on shore (it is Good Friday). By reaching the Mediterranean, the Nationalists have cut the Republic in half. The Republican government decides to remain in Barcelona. General Miaja is placed in supreme command of all central and southwest Spain.

April 16–17—Neville Chamberlain signs a treaty with Italy whereby Mussolini agrees to withdraw his troops from Spain *after* the war is over. The Spanish Republican government sends a horrified protest against this Italian admission that they are openly breaking the nonintervention pact and Britains acceptance of the fact. Winston Churchill calls the treaty, "A complete triumph for Mussolini, who gains our cordial acceptance for his fortification of the Mediterranean against us."

April 18—Tortosa falls to the Italians, but the fierce fighting there has exhausted them, and they are withdrawn from the front lines. The heavy rains begin in southern Spain. Roads become mires of mud; planes are grounded. Republican defenses stiffen and hold all along the line.

April 27—The Nationalist offensive, which had seemed to promise a speedy victory, has been halted all along the line. Frustrated Nationalists begin to murmur against General Franco. General Yagüe, in a public speech, has declared that the fighting qualities of the Republican troops are excellent. He refers to the Germans and Italians as "beasts of prey." Although he is temporarily relieved of his command for this indiscretion, many Nationalists share his views.

May 1—Premier Juan Negrín issues a declaration of Republican war aims. It is modeled after Woodrow Wilson's Fourteen Points, which were the basis for peace in the First World War. Negrín's Thirteen Points include expulsion of all foreign military forces, universal suffrage, no reprisals, protection of capitalist economy, guarantee of workers' rights, land reform and respect for regional liberties, general amnesty, and international cooperation through the League of Nations. Hereafter, Negrín will use the Thirteen Points as a basis for secret attempts to obtain a negotiated peace from Franco. But the Nationalists will discuss nothing but unconditional surrender.

May 13—In the United States heavy pressure has been brought upon the government to repeal the Embargo Act and sell arms to the Republic. Today Einstein and other scientists join with former Secretary of State Henry Stimson and Senator Gerald Nye in urging Cordell Hull to help the Republic. Hull agrees, but many American Catholics object violently. Nothing is done.

June 2–10—The Republican town of Granollers, twenty miles

from Barcelona, is heavily bombed by the Italians. Three hundred and fifty civilians, mostly women and children, are killed. The usual international protests pour into Rome. British ships in the Mediterranean are once more attacked by "unknown" (Italian) submarines. The government of Neville Chamberlain faces an uproar in the House of Commons. Fearing that Chamberlain, their greatest friend, may fall, the Italians call off their air and under-water attacks for the time being.

June 14–25—The Republican town of Castellón falls to the Nationalists—but only after prolonged and bitter resistance. Although they are only fifty miles north of Valencia, the Nationalist offensive can make no further headway. France closes her border again, and Franco publishes a law whereby the Germans are given the opportunity of buying up to forty percent interest in Spanish iron mines. The Germans are very dissatisfied with the terms of this law and the manner of its announcement. Franco

"British ships in the Mediterranean are once more attacked . . ."
The Union Jack waves lazily from a British destroyer as a cargo ship is bombed in Valencia harbor.

refuses to discuss the matter with the German ambassador.

June 27—The Russians, in agreement with the Germans, British, and French, accept a plan for the withdrawal of all foreign volunteers from Spain. None of the powers believes the plan will actually be carried out.

July 5—The Nationalist Army in the south opens an offensive to take Valencia. But its forces pressing down from the north are held by Republican forces who cannot be driven from their mountain positions.

July 18–23—Italian divisions, led by heavy tanks, break through the Republican lines south of Teruel. They advance seventy miles in five days under heavy air and artillery cover. Valencia is threatened by a general collapse along this front. Republican forces behind the extensive and heavy fortifications of the village of Viver hold the Italian advance. Bombing makes no impression on the defenders. Every Nationalist assault is broken by heavy machine gun fire. Valencia is saved as the Nationalist offensive crumbles. Twenty thousand Nationalists are casualties on this front in a matter of four days.

July 24—The Republican government proposes to counterattack the Nationalists along their thin salient to the sea. Under command of General Vicente Rojo, Republican forces prepare to attack along the river Ebro about seventy miles from the sea. A new "Army of the Ebro" has been formed under the command of Juan Modesto. It consists of 100,000 men, including the International Brigades. They will be supported by seventy-five batteries of artillery. To take the offensive with only a small store of military supplies, and with the French frontier recently closed again at Britain's insistence, is a daring policy. But the attack must be made to relieve Nationalist pressure on Valencia.

July 25—The Army of the Ebro, led by a unit of the Eleventh International Brigade, crosses the river on a wide front at midnight. Pontoon bridges and small boats are used for this maneuver.

The Nationalist forces, which consist of the Army of Morocco, once again commanded by General Yagüe, are taken completely by surprise. Nationalist battalions and regiments on the bank of the Ebro are surrounded. Many are forced to surrender, while others retreat. All the Nationalist-held villages on the Ebro are captured by dawn. The Republicans have established a huge bridgehead across the river. In the center of the front, Republican forces almost reach the town of Gandesa. They capture all the high ground around the town. Four thousand Nationalist prisoners have been taken on this first day of the Ebro offensive. In the meantime, General Franco has rushed up heavy reinforcements.

August 1—The Republicans assault Gandesa in a savage series of hand-to-hand combats. The Fifteenth International Brigade fights desperately to conquer Hill 481, called by them "the pimple." Many British and Americans fall in this bloody fighting.

August 2—The Republican offensive has stalled. The Nationalists keep Gandesa. The Republicans begin to dig in and fortify their positions, while Nationalist air attack commences with devastatingly effective dive-bombing.

August 9–14—While Franco's German advisors ask for more anti-aircraft ammunition from Berlin, Republican forces are warned they must not retreat. Officers who order a retreat without written orders from above are to be shot by their own men. Nationalist tactics are to concentrate artillery fire on one small sector of the front and then advance to take it. The battle has become an artillery duel.

August 15–19—Nationalist counterattacks are successful all along the line, but their advances are limited. High points in the mountains, after changing hands several times, are eventually surrendered by the Republicans. The battlefields swelter under intense heat; the men are everywhere reaching the point of complete exhaustion. Every day as many as two hundred Nationalist

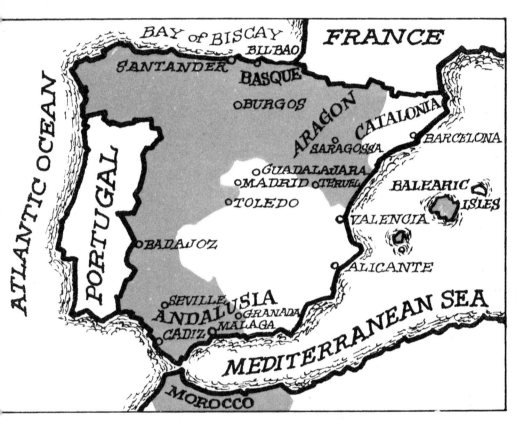

Spain, July, 1938 (Shaded areas indicate Nationalist regions)

"An average of 10,000 bombs per day are dropped."
Italian Savoia-Marchetti S-79 bombers unload over Valencia.

planes bomb and strafe the Republican lines. They meet no real resistance from the dwindling number of Republican aircraft and anti-aircraft batteries. An average of 10,000 bombs per day are dropped. But the Republican lines hold. The grim battle of heavy attrition along the banks of the Ebro goes on with neither side gaining any decisive advantage.

August 20–30—The Republic exults over the Ebro offensive. Although the attack has cost it mountains of precious war supplies, many thousands of dead and wounded, and has inflicted no serious harm on the Nationalists, it is counted a Republican victory because the small territorial gains are being held against Nationalist counterattack. The rest of Europe is growing fearful over the mounting crisis in Czechoslovakia. Britain and France fear Hitler will attack the Central European republic and thereby start a world war. Republican Spain is delighted by this crisis, since the Republicans believe a general war is the only way to defeat Franco. Nationalists grow alarmed for the same reason. Franco sends 20,000 prisoners to work on the fortification of the French frontier. Republicans have now agreed that the foreign volunteers should be withdrawn from Spain. For the Republic this will no longer entail a serious loss. Franco would be just as glad to be relieved of his inefficient Italian infantry. In any event the Germans and Italians do not intend to keep their part of the bargain, except superficially. The Republican successes at the Ebro have brought renewed gloom to Nationalist Spain. They infuriate Mussolini. On August 29 he shouts at Count Ciano, "Put on record in your diary, that today, August 29, I prophesy the defeat of Franco . . . The Reds are fighters, Franco is not!"

September—While the terrible battle along the Ebro continues, the English and French meet with Mussolini and Hitler in Munich. Bowing before Hitler's rages, English Prime Minister Neville Chamberlain and French Premier Edouard Daladier hand over the Republic of Czechoslovakia to Germany in hopes of obtaining "peace in our time." Chamberlain then suggests that the problem of Spain might be "solved" in the same way. The Russians finally lose hope of persuading France and Britain to join them in an anti-Hitler alliance. Therefore, they begin to consider the only other possible solution—an alliance with the Germans. As a result of this shift in Russian policy, aid to the Republic dwindles to nothing, and plans are made for the withdrawal of the International Brigades regardless of whether or not the Italians withdraw from Franco's side.

October 1—The Republic decides that, since the military importance of the International Brigades has lessened (their battalions are now largely filled with Spaniards, and their discipline and training have been imitated throughout the Republican Army), it will arrange for the departure of the Internationals under the League of Nations' supervision.

October 2—Premier Juan Negrín broadcasts a speech over the radio declaring that Spaniards must make peace. He asks the Nationalists whether they want to carry on the war until Spain is destroyed. The Nationalists remain adamant—they will discuss only unconditional surrender.

October 30–November 14—The main Nationalist counterattack of the battle of the Ebro begins. 175 batteries of artillery and bombardment by 100 planes precede an attack by several Army corps. The Republican lines are broken. On October 30, the entire Republican defense line crumbles. In the following days the Republican retreat becomes a rout as village after village falls to the Nationalists. By mid-November the Nationalists have regained all the ground they lost during the Republican offensive. The Republicans have lost 70,000 men on the Ebro, the Nationalists, 33,000. The Republic has also lost nearly all its aircraft and military supplies. In this one battle, the Republic loses its entire Army of the North.

November 15—A huge farewell parade is held in Barcelona

for the departing International Brigades. French, British, American, German, Italian, Belgian, Hungarian, Polish, and Canadian troops, veterans of the bloodiest battles of the Civil War, march down the Ramblas, while the population cheers and throws flowers. They are on their way home. *La Pasionaria* makes a speech in which she sums up the ideals both of Spanish Republicans and of all those who fought for their victory throughout the world. To the women of Barcelona she cries, "Mothers! Women! When the years pass and the wounds of war are staunched . . . then speak to your children. Tell them of the International Brigades. Tell them how, coming over seas and mountains, crossing frontiers bristling with bayonets . . . these men reached our country as crusaders for freedom. They gave up everything, their homes, their country . . . and they came and told us: 'We are here, your cause, Spain's cause, is ours. It is the cause of all advanced and progressive mankind.' Today they are going away. Many of them, thousands of them, are staying here with the Spanish earth for their shroud, and all Spaniards remember them with the deepest feeling." Then, turning to the Brigades, she declares, "You can go proudly. You are history. You are legend. You are the heroic example of democracy's solidarity and universality. We shall not forget you. The future may be black, but today is unforgettable in the life of the Republic."

XI

The Fall
of the
Republic

WHILE the citizens of Barcelona were cheering the departing International Brigades on November 15, 1938, the Nationalists were bringing to completion plans to strike a heavy blow against the Republic *immediately* after the battle of the Ebro, when Republican stocks of war matériel would be low. This would be possible only with heavy supplies of new equipment from Germany. But whereas the French frontier remained closed to the Republic and Russian supplies were kept from Republican ports by the Nationalist blockade, German and Italian supplies could flow freely to Franco. But would Hitler agree? Previously he, like the Russians, had followed a policy of not allowing his side to lose, but not supplying enough arms to ensure it a victory—which might provoke a general war.

General Franco, in order to ensure German support, now granted the Germans the increased participation in Spanish mining companies that they had long requested. Hitler then decided to re-equip the Condor Legion and send further heavy shipments of arms at once. Having taken the measure of Britain and France at Munich, the German dictator was now convinced that nothing he did in Spain would provoke a general war.

On the Republican side, the long agony along the banks of the Ebro inspired baseless optimism in November, 1938. The fact that it took the Nationalists three months to recapture territory the Republic had won in three days was held as proof of Republican staying power. But those who felt this way completely overlooked the fact that all Republican war supplies had been committed, and most lost, in that battle. And from where would new equipment come? Throughout the Republic, by the end of 1938, revolutionary zeal had subsided. Slogans now appealed more to patriotism and traditional Spanish virtues than to revolution. Food was terribly short in all Republican territories, but especially in the large cities. In Madrid the daily ration had fallen to two ounces of lentils or rice. In Barcelona, with its hundreds of thousands of refugees, conditions were even worse. And while the Republic continued to control most of Spain's industry, the output from factories, demoralized by Anarchist-Communist battles and lacking raw materials, fell alarmingly.

By the middle of December, 1938, with the arrival of heavy German supplies, General Franco was ready for his new offensive against Catalonia. All along the now quiet Ebro front, from the Pyrenees to the sea, the best Nationalist armies had been reorganized and redistributed. The Army of Urgel, under Muñoz Grandes, the Army of Maestrazgo under Valino, the Army of Aragon under Ituarte Moscardó, the Army of Navarre under José

Solchaga, and, finally, the Army of Morocco under Yagüe were placed into position for the offensive. With them was the Italian Littorio division (the other Italian divisions had been withdrawn from Spain during the preceding months). These Nationalist armies, numbering 300,000 men, were to be supported by more than 550 pieces of artillery and the newly refurbished Condor Legion.

Opposing this force, the Republic could muster in Catalonia only 220,000 men. These were divided into the Army of the East under Perea and the Army of the Ebro under Juan Modesto. The troops were almost without air and artillery support. They had few machine guns and very little ammunition left after the battle of the Ebro. Even rifles were in short supply. Besides, the men were exhausted. And if the civilians behind them remained confident, these troops knew the truth of their condition.

". . . the long agony along the banks of the Ebro had inspired baseless optimism." Loyalist trenches outside Madrid.

The Nationalist onslaught began on December 23, 1938. It was immediately successful everywhere against surprised and demoralized Republican defenders. Although Lister's Army Corps held out for two weeks in one sector, the heavy armor and superior equipment of the Nationalists soon told. On January 3 the front was broken wide open, and the Nationalists advanced as fast as their legs and wheels could carry them. With the fall of Tarragona to Yagüe on January 14, 1939, the way to Barcelona was open at last.

And now, when it was already too late, the French government once again opened its border for the passage of arms into Catalonia. Too late the Spanish Republican government ordered all men between the ages of seventeen and fifty-five to the colors, too late they seized control of Catalonia's flagging industries. Ill-prepared and ill-equipped counterattacks on other fronts had no effect on the Nationalist offensive.

Barcelona became a city of terror. Its hundreds of thousands of refugees now joined thousands from the city itself on another panic-stricken flight to safety. The French border was their last hope. Air raids on the city continued without letup. While thousands wandered hopelessly around the docks seeking non-existent passages on ships bound anywhere out of Spain, Nationalist planes subjected the port to heavy attack. Public administration broke down, and the streets were piled high with uncollected refuse. Scenes of indescribable misery engulfed the great capital city of Catalonia.

By January 14 the Nationalist armies had arrived at the river Llobregat, a bare five miles from Barcelona. Despite passionate appeals to make Barcelona another Madrid and the Llobregat another river Manzanares, Negrín's government, Communist leaders, trade union and political leaders, high ranking officers, all joined the refugees in fleeing towards the French border. Madrid's heroic defense was not to be repeated here. Months of starvation, years of violence, the civil war within the Civil War—all these had undermined the city's will to resist. Lawless mobs now appeared, to prowl the streets and loot abandoned shops.

On January 26, 1939, the triumphant Army of Morocco, led by General Yagüe, entered the city of Barcelona. Appropriately enough, a German-made tank was the first Nationalist vehicle into the city. While those of the working class who had not fled remained behind closed doors, Nationalist sympathizers appeared in the streets to greet their "liberators" with cheers and flowers. By mid-afternoon all the government buildings had been occu-

"The Nationalist onslaught began on December 23, 1939."

pied, and by evening the city was completely in Nationalist hands.

Meantime, on the roads leading north, five hundred thousand refugees fled blindly towards the French frontier. The overwhelming majority of these people had nothing to fear personally from the Nationalists—they were victims of mass hysteria. All the previous Republican evacuations—from Irún, Bilbao, Málaga— all these were as nothing compared to the flight from Catalonia. Thousands of cold, starving, miserable refugees, along with demoralized units of the Republican Army, clogged the roads. On the other hand, the refugees, in spite of their misery, never

Nationalist cavalry and planes attack towards Barcelona.

once lost dignity. Observers noted that all of them—men, women, and children—held their heads high as they walked to France.

The French government had at first, for financial reasons, refused to open its frontier to the refugees. They were completely unprepared to assume the burden of supporting the 250,000 civilians and 250,000 soldiers who craved admittance. But, by the end of January, the frontier was opened. And here Catalonia's tragedy reached its most intense moment of suffering. For the French had arranged reception camps for women and children— and other camps for men. Families were now separated and Republican soldiers disarmed. Under guard of French police the refugees were led to their new homes. There they were to receive a terrible disillusionment.

Most of the camps erected throughout southern France were no more than barbed wire entanglements surrounding vast areas of wasteland. There was no shelter, no food, no medical supplies, little water, and no sanitation. Hundreds died in these camps from untended wounds. The French appealed to other nations to help them with these refugees, but the world turned a deaf ear. Belgium agreed to take three thousand children and Britain and Russia each would take a small number of carefully selected leaders. But the vast mass of refugees had to choose between life in the camps or return to Nationalist Spain. The United States government did nothing. Although relief committees around the world raised funds to help those in the camps, the money was never sufficient. Eventually many of the refugees were to return to Spain. Many more, after France went to war, enlisted in the French Army; some melted away into the countryside of southern France (where they are still a large fraction of the population); but thousands remained in the camps—some to be victims of German revenge when France fell, others to wait until the end of World War Two for final freedom.

During these anguished days, the Nationalist Army continued

its advance on the heels of the fleeing Republicans up the coast towards France. By February 5 the Nationalists had captured Gerona, where some members of the Republican government had paused on their flight to Paris. By February 10, Nationalist armies held the French frontier at all points. The campaign in Catalonia was ended. It had not only been a mortal blow to the Republic but had brought to an end the ancient dream of Catalan independence. Catalan itself was banned as an official language, and the usual imprisonments and executions took place on a large scale.

The fall of Catalonia convinced the world that the Republic was defeated. While Nationalist credit soared on all the world's exchanges, that of the Republic sank to zero. The governments of Britain and France now made haste to recognize the Nationalists as Spain's official government. France sent an agent to Burgos to negotiate this with General Franco. On February 27, after the French had agreed to hand over all Spanish money, ships, and matériel held by them, and to recognize General Franco as Head of State, the Nationalists agreed to receive a French ambassador. This turned out to be Marshal Henri Pétain, who had fought alongside Franco many years before in Morocco and who was soon to head the shameful Vichy government that collaborated with Hitler after the fall of France.

Britain, at the urging of Republican representatives, tried at first to extract promises of a general amnesty and no reprisals as their condition for recognizing the Nationalist government. General Franco therefore sent a telegram to Neville Chamberlain in which he assured the Prime Minister that his patriotism, his honor as a gentleman, and his generosity were the best guarantees for an equitable and merciful peace in Spain. But, to continued Republican attempts to negotiate a surrender, he declared, "The Nationalists have won. The Republic must therefore surrender without conditions."

Later Franco announced that Nationalist courts would deal only with atrocity cases. Neville Chamberlain was apparently satisfied with these promises, and on February 27, 1939, the British government recognized the Nationalists as the government of Spain, and ambassadors were exchanged. When the matter was brought up in the House of Commons, Clement Attlee, leader of the Labor party, arose to say, "We see in this action a gross betrayal of democracy, the consummation of two and a half years of the hypocritical pretense of nonintervention and a connivance all the time at aggression. And this is only one step further

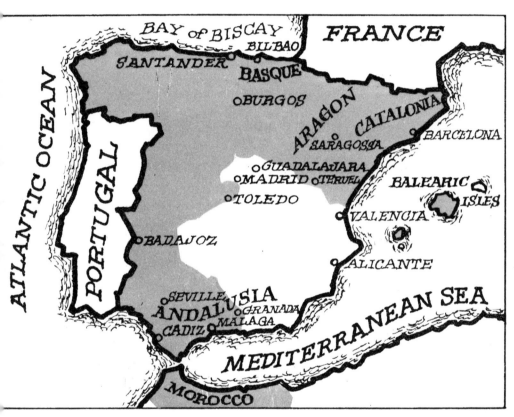

Spain, February, 1939 (Shaded areas indicate Nationalist regions)

in the downward march of His Majesty's government in which at every stage they do not sell, but give away the permanent interests of this country. They do not do anything to build up peace or stop war, but merely announce to the whole world that anyone who is out to use force can always be sure that he will have a friend in the British Prime Minister."

Russia, preparing her own great betrayal of her loudly proclaimed principles in the form of a non-aggression pact with Hitler, denounced what she called the falsity of "the capitalist policy of capitulation before the aggressor." She refused to recognize the National government—although she had long since decided to end her direct entanglement in Spain.

Other nations followed the British and French lead. The United States recognized the Nationalists on April 1, 1939.

While the world was rushing to abandon the Republic, Premier Juan Negrín and his government, accompanied by such Communist leaders as *La Pasionaria,* Modesto, and Lister, returned from France to Valencia. Since all attempts by Negrín to negotiate peace with the Nationalists had foundered on the rock of unconditional surrender, they had no choice but to continue the struggle. The Republic still held one-third of Spain and the great cities of Madrid, Valencia, and Alicante. The Republican Army still numbered 500,000 men. But there were almost no supplies for this fighting force. The Army around Madrid reported that it possessed only 95,000 rifles. Besides that, the civilian populations of Madrid and Valencia were starving. The Army officers in Madrid and Valencia, who had been out of touch with the government ever since it had gone to Barcelona, were weary of war and the futility of hopeless resistance. The only group in Spain that urged fighting on was the Communist party. It was Stalin's policy to keep Germany and Italy engaged in Spain as long as possible, while withdrawing all direct Russian support for the Republic.

Premier Negrín had long since been searching for ways to peace without the knowledge of his Communist supporters. The Republican generals, meanwhile, who had never had much sympathy for the Communists, now saw in them the main stumbling block to securing better terms from General Franco. Accordingly, under the leadership of Colonel Segismundo Casado in Madrid, a group of officers organized a plot to seize control of the remains of Republican Spain from the Negrín government. By so doing they felt they could negotiate better terms with the Nationalists, many of whom had been at one time brothers-in-arms. These officers were to achieve success primarily because of the support they received from the Anarchists, who now saw an opportunity to revenge themselves on the Communists.

Premier Negrín, sensing the conspiracy, flew to Madrid for an interview with Casado. The Colonel told him, truthfully enough, that the Army was without shoes, weapons, ammunition, or morale. The loss of Catalonia had cut Republican resources by seventy percent. As for the condition of the people in Madrid, Negrín could see for himself the mass starvation. The American Quaker Relief Committee estimated at this time that the stores of food in the capital would sustain life at a starvation level for only two more months. There were no medicines or medical supplies. Nevertheless, Negrín held a meeting of all high-ranking officers in the Madrid airport. There, on February 26, he told them of his attempts to make peace and of the rebuffs he had received. He asked for their opinions. Almost unanimously they were in favor of immediate surrender. Only old General Miaja urged continued resistance. Negrín returned to Valencia after issuing orders for a fight to the finish.

Meantime Colonel Casado continued to enlist officers in his attempt to end the war. "I can get more out of Franco than Negrín's government ever can," he announced. Except for the Communist officers, who were not informed of Casado's plans, the Colonel succeeded in gaining overwhelming support among the officers. These men now prepared to seize the governmental power and defend themselves against the almost certain Communist attack upon the plot. When preparations were complete, Colonel Casado addressed the Republic over Radio Madrid, asking for support. Premier Negrín immediately telephoned him from Valencia.

"What is going on in Madrid, my Colonel?" Negrín demanded.

"I have revolted," Casado informed him.

"Against whom? Against me?"

"Yes, against you."

Negrín told him he was acting insanely and hung up. But there was almost nothing the Premier could do about it.

Meanwhile, the Communists remained indecisive. Should they allow the defeatist nature of Casado's conspiracy to become more apparent before nipping it off with troops under their control? When the Communist Jesús Hernández sought advice from the Russian Military Mission at Valencia he found that headquarters in great confusion. Trunks and boxes were everywhere. Papers were being burned, and officers were packing frantically. In answer to his inquiries, General Borov, the head of the mission, simply muttered, "We are leaving, we are leaving."

Both Stalin and the Spanish Communists were surprised by the Casado conspiracy—but more surprised by its immediate success. Although certain Communist regiments in Madrid now started to move against Casado, the majority of Communist officers decided to join him. Negrín and his cabinet, as well as many of the Communist leaders, flew to Dakar in French West Africa, where they hopefully awaited news of Casado's defeat.

In the midst of this chaos, the Republican fleet, uncertain as to what it ought to do, finally sailed to the French North African port of Bizerta. There it was interned by the French and eventually turned over to the Nationalists.

On March 6, after having waited at the Dakar airfield for several hours for word from Madrid, Valencia, and Alicante, Juan Negrín, his government, and the Communist leaders gave up all hope when they learned that Alicante had gone over to Casado. At three in the afternoon they boarded planes and flew to France. Thus the last Republican government fled Spain. The Civil War, which had started with an uprising of Army officers, was to end the same way.

Some of the confused Communist units in Madrid opened fire on Casado's men. On March 7, 8, and 9, there was heavy firing and some street fighting in the capital. But by March 10 Casado was in complete control. His hastily formed National Council now quickly dispatched officers to Nationalist Headquarters to open unofficial negotiations for peace. But General Franco, who had been quietly reorganizing his powerful armies for a death blow at the moribund Republic, refused to make any concessions to Casado, just as he had to Negrín.

When it became clear to Casado that there was no hope of obtaining terms from the Nationalists, he immediately began to plan for the evacuation of his Army to Valencia. There transportation was to be organized for all Republicans who wished to flee abroad. He now saw that he had to gain as much time as possible for escape. On March 19, therefore, he opened formal negotiations with the Nationalists, hoping to delay and gain time. While talks dragged on, Republican leaders escaped to France and Africa.

On March 26, after the collapse of these negotiations, the Nationalist armies began to advance again. General Yagüe drove on Madrid through the Sierra Morena. By nightfall thirty thousand prisoners had been taken. On March 27, the Nationalists and Italians advanced on the capital from Toledo. But no battles were fought, for the Republican Army had decided in its rank and file to demobilize itself. Climbing out of their fortifications and trenches, the Republican soldiers happily embraced the

"Han pasado!" Republican refugees flee Madrid
just before the capital falls to Franco's Nationalists.

Nationalist troops facing them. Many Republican units went over to the enemy. But the overwhelming majority of Republican soldiers simply set aside their weapons, bade goodbye to their comrades, and went home. Colonel Casado and his National Council fled from Madrid to Valencia when the last Republican troops had vanished.

In the capital, Nationalist sympathizers who had been in hiding for nearly three years now emerged into the streets and organized a temporary municipal government. At noon on March 28, 1939, the Nationalist armies entered Madrid without a shot being fired. While they marched into the city and took over the government buildings, crowds of Nationalists on the streets shouted: "Han pasado!" (They have passed.)

Valencia, meanwhile, presented a picture of terrible confusion and panic. Nationalists went boldly about the streets giving the Falangist salute, while Republican leaders, trade union officials, Communists, ranking Army officers, and government officials fought for space on planes and ships leaving the doomed city. Colonel Casado broadcast an appeal for calm and then took passage in a British cruiser bound for France. Most other Republican leaders also made good their escape to France. On March 30, the Italians entered Alicante, and the Nationalists under General Aranda entered Valencia. During that day and the following, all the coastal villages fell into their hands. By April 1, 1939, resistance was at an end. From the Pyrenees to Gibraltar, from the Bay of Biscay to the Mediterranean, the war-torn land of Spain was at peace—conquered by the Nationalist movement of which General Francisco Franco was now the undisputed head.

Epilogue

AND so the Spanish Civil War flickered out amid betrayal, flight, and rejoicing. The world's attention, so deeply involved, and the world's passions, so bitterly aroused, were soon to be diverted to the events of the Second World War. Yet that war seemed, somehow, less emotionally important than the relatively small conflict in Spain. For on the Iberian Peninsula, the hopes and fears of two decades took actual, isolated, and distinct form and fought themselves out. The muddy waters of national greed, uneasy alliance, and fighting for mere survival that distinguished the Second World War, as they had the First, did not seem to apply to Spain. There men had fought for ideals.

Spain itself lay prostrate in the harsh heat of the summer of 1939. There were, according to Spanish sources, one million dead. Over two hundred thousand remained in prison. Untold millions of pounds' worth of property had been destroyed. Spain's railroads and most of its merchant marine were wrecked. Although the land had not suffered in the same way as northern France did from the trench, explosive, and gas warfare of 1914–1918, nevertheless the cities had been badly bombed, and more than one hundred and eighty towns were so completely destroyed that they were "adopted" by General Franco. That is, the Nationalist government undertook to rebuild them. Although Spanish industry was not heavily damaged during the war, it was now worn out, largely obsolete, and desperately starved for raw materials. While roads were in fair shape, hundreds of bridges had been destroyed. Everywhere the land was bare of livestock, and the flight of more than half a million refugees to foreign lands had depopulated whole districts of cities and entire villages.

The hatred, the idealism, the nobility, loyalty, treachery, and devotion of fifty years of Spanish history burned themselves out during the ferocious war struggle. The parties of the left—Anarchist, Communist, and Socialist—were now destroyed. Their ideals seemed somehow no longer relevant to Spanish conditions. Separatism, in both Catalonia and the Basque regions, was dead.

On the right, victory did not bring political success to any one group. Monarchists are still waiting for a restoration of King Alfonso's grandson to the throne, thirty years later. His prospects are indifferent. The Church, although it regained many of its old privileges, found in the years to come that it had to deal with a people who had lost much of their concern with religious matters. Anticlericalism, suppressed, expressed itself as simple indifference. The *Falange,* although it was to remain the only political party in Spain, found itself relegated to a subordinate position, its ideals largely unheeded. The Army is, of course, eternal in Spain.

Yet those Army leaders who had originally conspired with General Franco—Sanjurjo, Mola, and Goded—were all dead. Those who helped him win the victory—Yagüe, Queipo de Llano, Aranda, Dávila, and the rest—enjoyed high positions for a while but found themselves without effective power against the Head of State.

For three years, two different Spains fought for possession of their homeland. The Republic had held ideology paramount, but its political maturity had had little time to develop, and the essential economic and social conditions for democracy were lacking. It was defeated by an older Spain—one which, although based upon ancient, outmoded, and harshly repressive social and political principles, was nevertheless deeply rooted in the experience of Spanish history.

The Republican leaders who fled—Negrín, Prieto, Azaña, and the rest—set up various committees and a government in exile, basing themselves mainly upon the support of the Mexican government. But over the years their hopes, along with their funds, diminished. They are all dead now. Many of the Communist leaders, such as *El Campesino* and Jesús Hernández, were to quarrel with Stalin and leave the party. Some others—including *La Pasionaria*, Lister, and Modesto—remain today the nominal leaders of the almost nonexistent Spanish Communist party in exile.

The Facists and Nazis who intervened in Spain—Hitler, Mussolini, Ciano, and the others—met the violent deaths that had always been waiting for them. Chamberlain, Daladier, and the other appeasers died in disgrace and isolation. Stalin, Cordell Hull, and Anthony Eden were each to learn what temporizing with fascism could cost when their countries' time came on the Fascist schedule of conquest. The members of the International Brigades met various fates. For some time, those who had enlisted from Eastern Europe fell under Stalin's mad suspicions—presumably for having associated with non-Communists. Some among them were shot in various purges, others had to wait for Stalin's death for "political rehabilitation." French and English members shared their hard-bought military experience with their countries in the Second World War. American members of the Lincoln and Washington Battalions, however, fell under the deep suspicion of the United States Army during that struggle and were only sent overseas late in the fighting. With the rise of McCarthyism, they found themselves declared enemies of their country. Membership in almost any of the organizations set up to help the Republic was eventually to be declared "subversive" by the United States Department of Justice. The Italians who survived the battles of Spain were soon to fall in Albania, North Africa, and Italy itself, while the Germans of the Condor Legion were to meet their match in England's Royal Air Force.

If Hitler imagined that he had bought himself a firm ally by his sacrifices of German men and supplies in Spain, he was to receive a rude shock. Although in the early days of the war Spain allowed certain ports and airfields to be used by German planes and submarines, this soon came to an end. When Hitler demanded that General Franco allow him to send divisions through Spain for the conquest of Gibraltar, he met blank refusal. The two men met finally at Hendaye on the French border in 1940. General Franco proved obdurate to German demands. More than that—he insisted on taking his afternoon *siesta* after lunch and kept Hitler waiting—a remarkable event in the *Führer's* life. Later Hitler declared he would rather have several teeth pulled than have another such interview with Franco. Plans were made by the Germans for the invasion of Spain but never carried out, as Hitler drove his armies to their rendezvous with destiny in Russia. During this battle in the east, a Spanish volunteer division—the Blue Division—commanded by Muñoz Grandes, fought alongside the Germans. But this was all the aid Hitler received. Like for-

Francisco Franco

eigners of all political persuasions, he had misunderstood Francisco Franco.

The General, now styled *Generalísimo* by his followers, displayed the unique ability to endure and to govern. He is today almost the last survivor of the political maelstrom that swept the world from 1932 to 1945—certainly, apart from Salazar of Portugal, the only continuing head of state. His great political insight was demonstrated by his *tour de force* in successfully keeping Spain out of the Second World War, an action for which all Spaniards remain grateful to this day.

Many years later, it was revealed, in testimony given at Nuremberg and at the Eichmann trial in Jerusalem, that those Jewish refugees from Nazi persecution who managed to cross the Spanish frontier found a safe sanctuary within Spain. Spanish inmates (Jewish or otherwise) of German concentration camps often remained relatively untouched by the Nazis, due, in large part, to the continuous barrage of protests from the Spanish government. On the other hand, Republican political leaders could expect little mercy from the *Generalísimo*. Thus, Luis Companys, the former president of the autonomous Catalan government, who had fled into exile in France, was later handed over to the Spanish Nationalists by the Pétain government of France and, on Franco's orders, shot. Only in 1945—six and one-half years after the end of the Civil War—was an amnesty declared for "political offenses" (i.e. Republicanism) by the Nationalist regime, but political prisoners continued to languish in Nationalist prisons as late as 1950.

With the growing certainty of Allied victory in the Second World War, Franco, as early as 1943, began to make some concessions to foreign liberal opinion. Thus the label of fascism was dropped as a description of the Nationalist state and the term "organic democracy" used in its place. In March of 1943 a pseudo *Cortes* was convened in Madrid. Its members were partly appointed and partly elected, under a system of strictly controlled suffrage, and, in any event, had no real power whatsoever. Likewise, as a sop to foreign opinion, the *Falange* was allowed to sink into obscurity until, in 1945, Franco could announce that no single Falangist was to be found in the Spanish cabinet, while the party itself no longer wielded any political power in Spain. This statement, obviously intended for foreign consumption, was later contradicted many times by the *Generalísimo* himself.

Franco's re-establishment of the Catholic Church as a dominant force in Spanish life, through the restoration of religious education, of state financial support for the Church, and by the repeal of Republican anticlerical laws, led in 1941 to a working arrangement with the Vatican that was finally formalized by a treaty in 1953.

These measures, however, did not serve to protect the Franco regime from the severe censure of the Allies after the Second World War. In July, 1945, Spain found herself branded by the Potsdam Declaration as unfit to associate with the United Nations. In December, 1946, the United Nations formally ostracized the Spanish government and recommended that all its member nations withdraw their ambassadors from Madrid. Thus Spain found itself practically friendless in the postwar world, with only the dictatorships of Portugal and Argentina still lending the Nationalist regime their support.

But foreign condemnation proved to have the opposite effect in Spain from what was intended. Spanish opinion rallied to the defense of the Franco government—partly from distaste for foreign interference and partly from fear of the upheaval that might result from Franco's downfall. Other governments were forced to recognize the failure of their policy, and one by one the foreign ambassadors returned to Madrid. The United States, in need now of European bases for its growing cold war with the Soviet Union, opened negotiations with the Franco regime for the construction of Strategic Bomber Command airfields in Spain in 1951. After two years of protracted bargaining, a defense agreement was signed by the United States and Spain on September 26, 1953. For the use of these bases the *Generalisimo* exacted a price in economic and military aid that has amounted, over the years, to more than 300 million pounds. And, with American support, Spain was finally admitted to the United Nations in 1955.

In 1947, the Nationalist regime announced a new "law of succession." Under its provisions, Spain was once again declared to be a kingdom. In the absence of a king, General Franco was to continue to exercise supreme power. His successor, of royal blood, would be required to swear support for Nationalist laws passed since the downfall of the Republic and fidelity to the principles of the *Falange* movement. In 1954 Franco signed an agreement with Don Juan, third son of Alfonso XIII and direct heir to the Spanish throne, that Don Juan's eldest son, Don Juan Carlos, should receive his education in Spain, thereby indicating his preference for Don Juan Carlos as a possible successor.

Meanwhile, the Nationalist regime in Spain continued to rest on authority and not on consent. But that authority was exercised with caution. Thus, although freedom of the press remained non-existent, freedom of association could bring severe penalties, and freedom of speech was carefully controlled, public order was maintained, foreign adventures were avoided (the granting of independence to Spanish Morocco in 1956 ended the last chapter in the history of Spanish imperialism), and a thoroughgoing and widespread system of social security for workers and their dependents was instituted. Besides that, with American help, large-scale economic developments were undertaken.

Nor was General Franco's caution derived only from the lessons to be learned in the downfall of Mussolini and Hitler. It was rather an expression of the man himself. During the Civil War he once replied to a German general's plea for haste: "Franco does not make war on Spain. He liberates Spain. I cannot destroy a single enemy, nor towns, nor any part of the countryside, nor industries, nor centers of production. For that reason, I cannot hurry. If I were in a hurry, I would be conducting myself like a foreigner . . . do not make me hasten, because that would mean killing a large number of Spaniards."

Today Spain remains, as she has remained for centuries, a land of extremes and contradictions. Electric power developments and experimental atomic reactor stations are to be found within walking distance of villages sunk in almost medieval ignorance and poverty. Huge and garish tourist hotels, as modern and well-appointed as any in the world, crowd the Mediterranean coastline, while only a few miles inland peasants toil on the large estates under semi-feudal conditions. While foreign investment establishes the latest in complex and modern factories to produce everything from automobiles to tranquilizers, Spain's illiteracy rate continues to be the highest in Europe.

Politically, the only useful definition of Spanish life continues to be "authoritarian." And, yet, as the generation that exhausted its political fervors in the Civil War vanishes from the scene, a new generation shows increasing signs of political awakening. Thus, the use of the strike has once again become a weapon in the hands of workers. In recent years the miners of Asturias, as well as dockyard workers in Bilbao and factory workers elsewhere in Spain, have resorted to strikes to improve their conditions. Nor is the government, either from fear of the consequences or perhaps belated recognition of the justice of their demands, disposed to employ as heavy a hand in suppressing strikes as once it would have shown. Most strikes now end in negotiations and compromise. Among the university students of Madrid and Barcelona, too, the stirrings of new political life can be seen. Student protest marches—usually ending in bloody clashes with the police and the imprisonment of student leaders—have become predictable phenomena in Spanish life.

But these signs of a rebirth of political consciousness must not be interpreted as a widespread will to revolution. The disillusionments of the Civil War are still too familiar to most Spaniards to permit their enthusiastic engagement on behalf of any political party, slogan, or battle cry whatsoever. And with the passage of the years, the old political solutions have come to seem irrelevant to Spanish needs. The rising class of leaders in Spain are today more interested in economic and social realities than political theories. Above all, they are determined to avoid the dreadful blood bath of another civil war. In this determination they are fulfilling a prophecy and a hope made during the fiercest days of the Civil War by Manuel Azaña, President of the Republic:

"When the torch passes to other hands, to other men, to other generations, let them remember, if they ever feel their blood boil and the Spanish temper is once more infuriated with intolerance, hatred, and destruction, let them think of the dead, and listen to their lesson: the lesson of those who have bravely fallen in battle, generously fighting for a great ideal, and who now, protected by their maternal soil, feel no hate or rancor, and who send us with the sparkling of their light, tranquil and remote as that of a star, the message of the eternal Fatherland which says to all its sons: Peace, Pity, and Pardon."

Bibliography

The Spanish Civil War aroused passions and consciences that have made it one of the most thoroughly documented struggles in history. Primary sources, including documents, the memoirs of those who took part, and reports by various official organizations, are usually in Spanish. Where they have been translated they are often difficult to come by for the general reader. Therefore a special suggested reading section will be found at the end of the bibliography which may prove of more practical use to most readers.

AGUIRRE Y LECUBE, JOSÉ, *De Guernica a Nueva York Pasando por Berlin* (Buenos Aires, 1944).

ALONSO GONZALEZ, BRUNO, *La Flota Republicana y La Guerra Civil en España* (Mexico City, 1944).

ALVAREZ DEL VAYO, JULIO, *Freedom's Battle* (New York, 1940); *The Last Optimist* (New York, 1950).

"ANDRÉS DE PALMA," *Mallorca en la Guerra Contra el Marxismo* (Palma de Mallorca, 1936).

ARALAR, J., *La Rebelión Militar Española y el Pueblo Vasco* (Buenos Aires, 1937).

ARAQUISTAIN QUEVEDO, LUIS, *El Comunismo y La Guerra de España* (Carmaux, 1939).

AUTHORS TAKE SIDES—Pamphlet published in London, 1937.

AZANA Y DIAZ, MANUEL, *Memorias Intimas* (Madrid, 1939).

BORKENAU, FRANZ, *The Spanish Cockpit* (Faber, 1937).

BRENAN, GERALD, *The Spanish Labyrinth* (Cambridge University Press, 1943).

BRERETON, G., *Inside Spain* (Quality Press, 1938).

BROWDER, EARL, *Next Steps to Win the War in Spain* (New York, 1938).

BUCKLEY, H., *Life and Death of the Spanish Republic* (Hamish Hamilton, 1940).

CAMPOAMOR, CLARA, *La Révolution Espagnole vue par une Ré-publicaine* (Paris, 1937).

CASADO, SEGISMUNDO, *The Last Days of Madrid* (Peter Davies, 1939).

CASTILLEJO, J., *Education and Revolution in Spain* (Oxford University Press, 1937).

CATTELL, DAVID C., *Communism and the Spanish Civil War* (Cambridge University Press, 1955); *Soviet Diplomacy and the Spanish Civil War* (Cambridge University Press, 1958).

CLERGE BASQUE, LE—Pamphlet published in Paris, 1938.

COLLECTIVE LETTER OF THE SPANISH BISHOPS ON THE WAR IN SPAIN—Pamphlet published in London, 1937.

COT, PIERRE, *The Triumph of Treason* (New York, 1944).

COWLES, VIRGINIA, *Looking for Trouble* (Hamish Hamilton, 1941).

COX, GEOFFREY, *Defence of Madrid* (Gollancz, 1937).

DIARIO DE SESIONES DE LAS CORTES ESPANOLES—Official record of sessions, available in the Cortes Library, Madrid.

DIAZ, JOSÉ, *Lessons of The Spanish War 1936–9* (London 1940).

DUNDAS, LAWRENCE, *Behind the Spanish Mask* (Robert Hale, 1943).

FEIS, HERBERT, *The Spanish Story* (New York, 1948).

FERNSWORTH, LAWRENCE, *Spain's Struggle for Freedom* (Boston, 1958).

FISCHER, LOUIS, *Men and Politics* (Cape, 1941).

FOLTZ, CHARLES, *The Masquerade in Spain* (Boston, 1948).

FOX, RALPH, *A Writer in Arms* (Lawrence & Wishart, 1937).

FRANCO, FRANCISCO, *Palabras* (Burgos, 1938).

GARCIA-VALINO Y MARCEN, RAFAEL, *Guerra de Liberación Española* (Madrid, 1949).

GARRATT, G. T., *Mussolini's Roman Empire* (Penguin Books, 1938).

GENERAL CAUSE, THE—Report of the mass lawsuit brought by Nationalist authorities, trans. Madrid, 1953.

GERAHTY, CECIL, *The Road to Madrid* (Hutchinson, 1937).

GERMANY AND THE SPANISH CIVIL WAR, 1936–1939—Vol. III of the *Documents on German Foreign Policy* (His Majesty's Stationery Office, 1951).

GONZALEZ, VALENTIN (*El Campesino*), *Listen Comrades!* (Heinemann, 1953).

GREENE, HERBERT, *Secret Agent in Spain* (Robert Hale, 1938).

GROSSI, MANUEL, *La Insurrección de Asturias* (Valencia, 1935).

HAMILTON, THOMAS J., *Appeasement's Child* (Gollancz, 1943).

HENRIQUEZ CAUBIN, JULIAN, *La Batalla del Ebro* (Mexico City, 1944).

HERNANDEZ TOMAS, JESUS, *Yo fui un Ministro de Stalin* (Mexico City, 1953).

IBARRURI, DOLORES (*La Pasionaria*), *Speeches* (Lawrence & Wishart, 1939); *They Shall Not Pass* (Lawrence & Wishart, 1967).

IN SPAIN WITH THE INTERNATIONAL BRIGADES—Pamphlet published in London, 1938.

INTERNATIONAL BRIGADES, THE—Pamphlet published by the Nationalist Government in Madrid, 1953.

IRIBARREN, JOSÉ, *El General Mola* (Madrid, 1945).

KERSHNER, H., *Quaker Service in Modern War* (New York, 1950).

KNICKERBOCKER, H. R., *The Siege of the Alcázar* (Hutchinson, 1936).

KOESTLER, ARTHUR, *Spanish Testament* (Gollancz, 1937).

LARGO CABALLERO, FRANCISCO, *Mis Recuerdos* (Mexico City, 1954).

LEAGUE OF NATIONS—*Official Journal for the Years 1936–1939*.

LIZARRA, A., *Los Vascos y La República Española* (Buenos Aires, 1944).

MARTIN BLAZQUEZ, JOSÉ, *I Helped to Build an Army* (Secker & Warburg, 1939).

MATTHEWS, HERBERT, *Two Wars and More to Come* (New York, 1938); *The Education of a Correspondent* (New York, 1946); *The Yoke and the Arrows* (Heinemann, 1958).

MENÉNDEZ PIDAL, R., *The Spaniards in Their History* (New York, 1950).

MORA, CONSTANCIA DE LA, *In Place of Splendour* (Michael Joseph, 1940).

NELSON, STEVE, *The Volunteers* (New York, 1953).

O'DUFFY, E., *Crusade in Spain* (Dublin, 1938).

ORLOV, ALEXANDER, *The Secret History of Stalin's Crimes* (Jarrolds, 1954).

ORWELL, GEORGE, *Homage to Catalonia* (Secker & Warburg, 1938).

PADELFORD, N. J., *International Law and Diplomacy in the Spanish Civil Strife* (Macmillan, 1939).

PARLIAMENTARY DEBATES OF THE HOUSE OF COMMONS, 1936–39 (His Majesty's Stationery Office).

PAUL, ELLIOT, *The Life and Death of a Spanish Town* (Peter Davies. 1939).

PRIETO, INDALECIO, *Yo y Moscú* (Madrid, 1955).

PRIMO DE RIVERA, JOSÉ ANTONIO, *Obras Completas* (Madrid, 1954).

REGLER, GUSTAV, *The Owl of Minerva* (Rupert Hart-Davis, 1959).

REPORT OF THE SUB-COMMITTEE ON THE SPANISH QUESTION—*U.N. Security Council Report* issued in New York, 1946.

ROGERS, F. T., *Spain: A Tragic Journey* (New York, 1937).

ROJO, VICENTE, *España Heroica!* (Buenos Aires, 1942).

ROLFE, EDWIN, *The Lincoln Battalion* (New York, 1939).

SALTER, CEDRIC, *Try-Out in Spain* (New York, 1943).

SHEEAN, VINCENT, *Not Peace, but a Sword* (New York, 1939).

SOUCHY, AUGUSTINE, *The Tragic Week in Barcelona* (Barcelona, 1937).

SPENDER, STEPHEN, *World Within World* (Hamish Hamilton, 1951).

STRONG, ANNA LOUISE, *Spain in Arms* (New York, 1937).

TAYLOR, F., *The United States and the Spanish Civil War* (New York, 1956).

THOMAS, HUGH, *The Spanish Civil War* (Eyre & Spottiswoode, 1961).

TOGLIATTI, PALMIRO, *The Spanish Revolution* (New York, 1936).

WATSON, K., *Single to Spain* (Arthur Barker, 1937).

WEIZSACKER, ERNST VON, *Memoirs* (Gollancz, 1951).

WOOLF, BERTRAM D., *Khrushchev and Stalin's Ghost* (New York, 1957).

Suggested Reading

ÁLVAREZ DEL VAYO, JULIO, *Freedom's Battle* (New York, 1940); *The Last Optimist* (New York, 1950).

BORKENAU, FRANZ, *The Spanish Cockpit* (Faber, 1937).

BRENAN, GERALD, *The Spanish Labyrinth* (Cambridge University Press, 1943); *The Face of Spain* (Turnstile Press, 1950; Hamish Hamilton, 1957).

CIANO, COUNT GALEAZZO, *Diaries* (New York, 1946).

GIRONELLA, JOSÉ, *The Cypresses Believe in God* (New York, 1955).

HEMINGWAY, ERNEST, *For Whom the Bell Tolls* (Cape, 1941); *The Fifth Column and Other Plays* (Cape, 1939).

KOESTLER, ARTHUR, *Spanish Testament* (Gollancz, 1937); *The Invisible Writing* (Collins, 1954).

MALRAUX, ANDRÉ, *Man's Hope* (New York, 1938).

MENÉNDEZ PIDAL, R., *The Spaniards in Their History* (New York, 1950).

MORA, CONSTANCIA DE LA, *In Place of Splendour* (Michael Joseph, 1940).

ORWELL, GEORGE, *Homage to Catalonia* (Secker & Warburg, 1938).

PAUL, ELLIOT, *The Life and Death of a Spanish Town* (Peter Davies, 1939).

REGLER, GUSTAV, *Owl of Minerva* (Rupert Hart-Davis, 1959)

SENDER, RAMÓN, *Seven Red Sundays* (Faber, 1936).

SHEEAN, VINCENT, *Not Peace, But a Sword* (New York, 1939).

SPENDER, STEPHEN, *World Within World* (Hamish Hamilton, 1951); and LEHMANN, JOHN (editors), *Poems for Spain* (Hogarth Press, 1939).

THOMAS, HUGH, *The Spanish Civil War* (Eyre & Spottiswoode, 1961).

WINTRINGHAM, TOM, *English Captain* (Faber, 1939).

Index

Abd-el-Krim, 28, 29
Aguirre, José, 137
Air Force, Republican, 75, 86–7, 161, 172, 182
Albacete, 74
Alcalá Zamora, Niceto, 30, 32, 34, 36, 41
Alcázar, the, 63, 90–1, 130
Alfonso XII, King, 19
Alfonso XIII, King, 19, 28, 29, 30, 32, 36, 111, 202, 208
Algeciras, 53, 61, 64, 86
Alhama, 122
Alicante, 62, 63, 97, 112, 194, 199
Almería, 123
American troops, 127–8, 160, 171
Anarchists, 25, 26, 31, 34, 36, 41, 44, 55–6, 64, 79, 83, 85, 86, 91, 108, 114, 115, 124, 185, 195, 202; in Barcelona, 153–6; in Castilblanco, 34, 36; in government, 96, 100, 158; in Madrid, 44, 104–5; in Valencia, 153
Andalusia, 10, 28, 32, 51, 53, 54, 61, 64, 77, 86, 114, 115, 122, 124, 150
Andujar, 150
Anual, 28
Aragon, 60, 63, 143, 171–3
Aranda, Colonel Antonio, 60, 164, 167, 174, 199, 203
Argentina, 207
Aristocracy, 23, 28
Army, Regular, 28, 34, 64, 202–3; and Alfonso XII, 19; and Anarchists, 25; in Barcelona, 57–8; and the Church, 27; and idea of Republic, 22; and Franco, 113, and Isabella II, 18; in Morocco, 48–50; and Primo de Rivera, 30; and rebellion of 1820, 17; and rebellion of 1934, 39–40; and rebellion of 1936, 48–51; and Republic of 1931; 31, 32; and Republic of 1936, 41–2, 46; and separatists, 56
Army of Africa, 46, 50, 61, 64, 70, 80, 82–4, 95, 103, 104, 105, 122, 124, 168
Army of Aragon, 185
Army of the East, 186
Army of the Ebro, 177, 186
Army of Maestrazgo, 185
Army of Morocco, 46, 47, 61, 86, 91, 130, 167, 178, 186, 188; at Anual, 28; at Madrid, 83, 104, 105, 125–7; at Seville, 53, 82

Army of Navarre, 185
Army, Republican, 62, 77, 79, 84, 85, 86, 88, 102, 103, 110, 115, 137, 171, 172, 194, 197, 199; at the Alcázar, 90–1; at Badajoz, 82–3; at Brunete, 160–1; at Guadalajara, 131–3; at Madrid, 97, 124–5, 127; at Málaga, 122–4; at Santa María de la Cabeza, 150–2; at Teruel, 164–8, 171. *See also* Republicans
Army of Urgel, 185
Asensio, Colonel Carlos, 82, 95
Astray, General Millán, 118–19
Asturias, 60, 63, 88, 209; and miners' rebellion, 39–40
Atrocities, 64–6, 111, 192
Attlee, Clement, 192, 194
Auden, W. H., 74
Avila, 39
Azaña, Manuel, 32, 34, 36, 55, 97–9, 159, 210; and Largo Caballero, 95, 157; and Prieto, 173; and post-war government, 203

Badajoz, 82–3
Balboa, Vasco, 11
Baldwin, Stanley, 69, 129, 138
Balearic Islands, 57, 86
Barcelona, 10, 12, 23, 26, 39, 63, 77, 117, 137, 169, 172–4, 182–4, 194, 209; and air raids, 163; Communists in, 153–7, 173; fall of, 187–9; 1937 crisis in, 153–6; rebellion in, 56–8; and refugees, 172, 185; War Council at, 173–4
Basques, 10, 17, 31, 34, 56, 60, 63–4, 86, 111, 114, 118, 134, 149; and autonomy, 27–8, 135–7; and the Church, 111, 137, 146; and end of independence, 148–9, 202; at Irún, 85; and Nationalist offensive, 134 ff; origins and character of, 135–7; and refugees, 143, 148; and Santander campaign, 146–8
Bayo, Captain Alberto, 86, 87
Bebb, Captain, 45, 46, 48, 50, 69
Beckett, Samuel, 75
Belchite, 171
Belgium, 190
Beorlegui, Colonel Alfonso, 85–6
Bermeo, 142

efforts of, 182, 194–5; in postwar era,
203; and request for French aid,
172, 173; war aims of, 175; at War
Council, Barcelona, 173
Neutrality Act of 1935 (U.S.), 73, 146
NKVD in Spain, 115
Nonintervention, 69–70, 128, 129–30, 146,
163
Nye, Senator Gerald, 175

O'Casey, Sean, 75
Ochandiano, 138
Oviedo, 39, 60, 88

Pamplona, 60
Pasionaria, La (Dolores Ibarruri), 42, 54,
79, 80, 100, 153, 169, 173, 183, 194,
203
Pavlov, General, 99, 127, 131, 132
Peasants, 14, 23, 24, 27, 28, 31, 34–5, 39,
41, 51, 55, 56, 64, 65, 114, 115, 117,
·155, 171, 209
Pemán, José María, 110–11
Perea, Major, 79, 186
Pétain, Marshal Henri, 192, 206
Philip II, 11, 14
Physical features of Spain, 9–10
Picasso, Pablo, 11, 142
Pinilla, Colonel, 88
Pius XI, 111, 146
Pizarro, Francisco, 11, 13
Polish troops, 102, 105, 106
Popular Front, Spanish, 41
Portugal, 207
Postwar conditions, Spain, 113–14, 201 ff.
Potsdam Declaration, 207
Pound, Ezra, 75
Pozas, General Sebastián, 124
Prieto, Indalecio, 55, 96, 155, 158; Com-
munist campaigns against, 169; and
plan to bomb German fleet, 159; in
postwar era. 203; at War Council,
Barcelona, 173–4
Prim, General Juan, 18
Primo de Rivera, José Antonio, 42, 43,
157; as founder of *Falange*, 37; and
trial by Republicans, 112–13
Primo de Rivera, General Miguel, 29, 30,
41
Puigdendolas, Colonel Ildefonso, 82

Queipo de Llano, General Gonzalo, 51–3,
120, 203
Quijorna, 161
Quiroga, Santiago Casares, 41, 42, 50, 56,

64; government of, 53–5

Refugees, 85, 123, 143, 148, 152, 172, 185,
187, 189–90, 191, 202, 206
Religion, 11, 12, 14, 27, 33, 110
Republic of 1873, 18
Republic of 1931, 30, 31
Republicans, the, 28, 30, 32, 34–6, 40–1,
50, 57, 61–2, 64–6, 75–7, 82, 84, 137,
139, 143, 152, 172; aid to, 69–70, 72–
3, 96–7, 128; at Barcelona, 58, 156,
174; and bombing of German ship,
158–9; and constitution, 32–3; and
Ebro offensive, 177–8, 181, 184–5;
and final defeat, 199; and France, 69–
70, 72, 96, 128, 197; and Madrid, 50,
159–60; at Málaga, 53; and religion,
111; and social developments, 116–17;
and Teruel, 164, 177; and the United
States, 73, 96–7; and Valencia crisis,
153, 177; war aims of, 175. *See also*
Air Force, Army, Navy, Republican
Rey, D'Harcourt, Colonel, 164–7
Riffs, the, 18, 28, 47
"Ring of Iron", Bilbao, 137, 143, 144
Riquelme, General Manuel, 83
Roatta, General Mario, 122, 123, 131
Roberts, Captain W. H., 139–40
Robles, *see* Gil Robles
Rojo, General Vicente, 177
Romerales, General Quintero, 49, 50
Ronda, 123
Roosevelt, Franklin D., 73
Rudilla, 171
Russia, 26, 68, 73, 80, 177, 196, 207; and
aid to Republicans, 72, 97, 99, 100,
113, 126–7, 153, 159, 163, 167, 173,
174, 184; and German alliance, 182;
and nonintervention agreement, 128–
30; and nonrecognition of National
government, 194; and refugees, 190;
and Revolution, 84, 103

Salamanca, 109, 113, 118
San Sebastián, 60, 84, 86
Sanjurjo, General José, 36, 42, 46, 50;
death of, 109, 203
Santa María de la Cabeza, 150–2
Santander, 144; campaign of, 146–8
Santona, 148
Sarabia, General Hernández, 164
Saragossa, 16, 60, 79, 164
Seguí, Colonel Almuzara, 49
Separatism, 27, 31, 34, 36, 39, 56, 118, 202
Serra, Father Junípero, 11

Seville, 13, 36, 51–3, 64, 77, 82, 86, 110, 151
Seville, Duke of, 120–3
Sirval, Luis, 40
Socialists, 25–6, 55, 64; and Anarchists, 25–6; and Asturian miners, 39; in Barcelona, 153; and Basques, 114, 136–7; and Communists, 95–6; and elections of 1931, 32; and France, 69; and labour unions, 44; and Popular Front, 41; post-war, 202; and Republicans, 30, 77
Solchaga, General José, 185–6
Sotelo, Calvo, 41, 44, 48
Stalin, Josef, 68, 72, 73, 159, 196; and policy in Spain, 194; in postwar era, 203–4; and purges, 68, 114
Stern, Lazar, see Kléber, General
Stimson, Henry, 175
Strikes, 25, 31, 39, 51, 53, 110, 209

Talavera de la Reina, 83
Tardienta, 77, 79
Tarragona, 187
Tella, Cantos, 82
Tella, General Heli Rolando de, 95, 101
Teruel, 164–8, 171, 177
Tetuán, 50
Thirteen Points, Negrín's, 175
Tito, Marshal, 75
Togliatti, 75
Toledo, 62–3, 88, 90–1, 197
Torrado, General, 97
Torremolinos, 122
Tortosa, 174, 175
Tremp, 174
Trotskyists, 26, 114, 153, 155, 156
Trubía, 39
Turón, 39

Ulbricht, W., 75
Ulíbarri, General Gamir, 147
Unamuno, Miguel de, 118–19
United Nations, 207
United States, 19, 22, 96–7, 146, 175, 190, 195, 204; and Neutrality Act (1936), 73; and recognition of Nationalist Government, 194; and Spanish air bases, 207

Valencia, 10, 63, 117, 197; fall of, 199; and Málaga offensive, 122, 123, 124; and Nationalist offensive, 177;

Republican Government in, 122, 134, 143, 153, 155, 156, 194; and Teruel offensive, 167, 168
Valladolid, 60
Varela, General José, 86, 91, 164–5; at siege of Madrid, 94, 97, 101, 102, 104, 105, 107, 161
Vega, General, 174
Velásquez, 11, 111
Victor Emmanuel, King, 29
Vigo, 10, 61, 64
Villa-Abraille, General, 52
Villafranca, 161
Villalba, Colonel, 122, 123, 124
Vinaroz, 174
Viver, 177
Vizcaya, 138
Volunteers, foreign, in Spain, 72–5, 102, 105, 127, 160, 171; British, 73, 125–6; Communist, 73–5; of the Fifth Regiment, 79–80; French, 74, 85, 86, 102; German, 72, 74; Italian, 71, 74; leaders of, 74–5. See also International Brigades

Warships: British, 138, 140, 163, 171, 176; German, 123, 158–9; Italian, 163; Nationalist, 84, 114, 123, 138–40, 143, 171; Republican, 53, 58, 61, 64, 80, 123, 124, 156, 196
Waugh, Evelyn, 75
Wellington, Arthur Wellesley, 1st Duke of, 16
West Rebecca, 75
Workers, industrial, 60, 64, 65, 114, 115; and arms, 50, 54–6, 58; in Barcelona, 58, 155; and the Church, 27; under Franco, 208; and ideas of revolution, 28; in Madrid, 54–6, 62; and poverty, 23; and rebellion of 1934, 39; and rebellion of 1936, 41; and socialism, 24; and strikes, 39, 51
World Wars I and II, 54, 67, 68, 93, 103, 113, 175, 190, 201, 204, 205, 206, 207

Yagüe, General Juan de, 82–3, 90, 94, 168, 169, 178, 186, 203; at Barcelona, 172, 175, 188; at Madrid, 94, 101, 197; at Tarragona, 187; at Teruel, 167–8, 171

Zamora, Niceto Alcalá, 30, 34, 36, 41
Zaro, Lieutenant Juan, 49